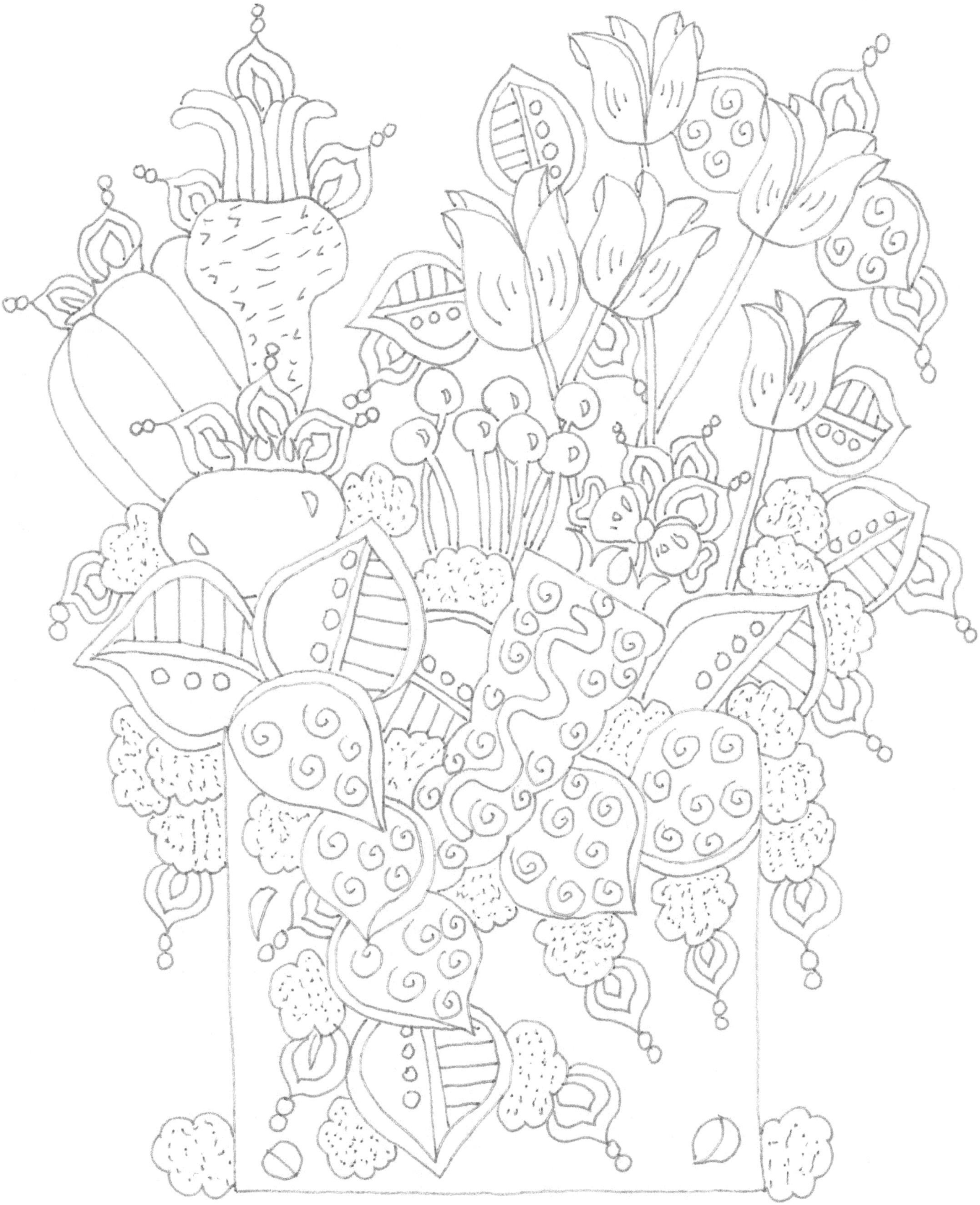

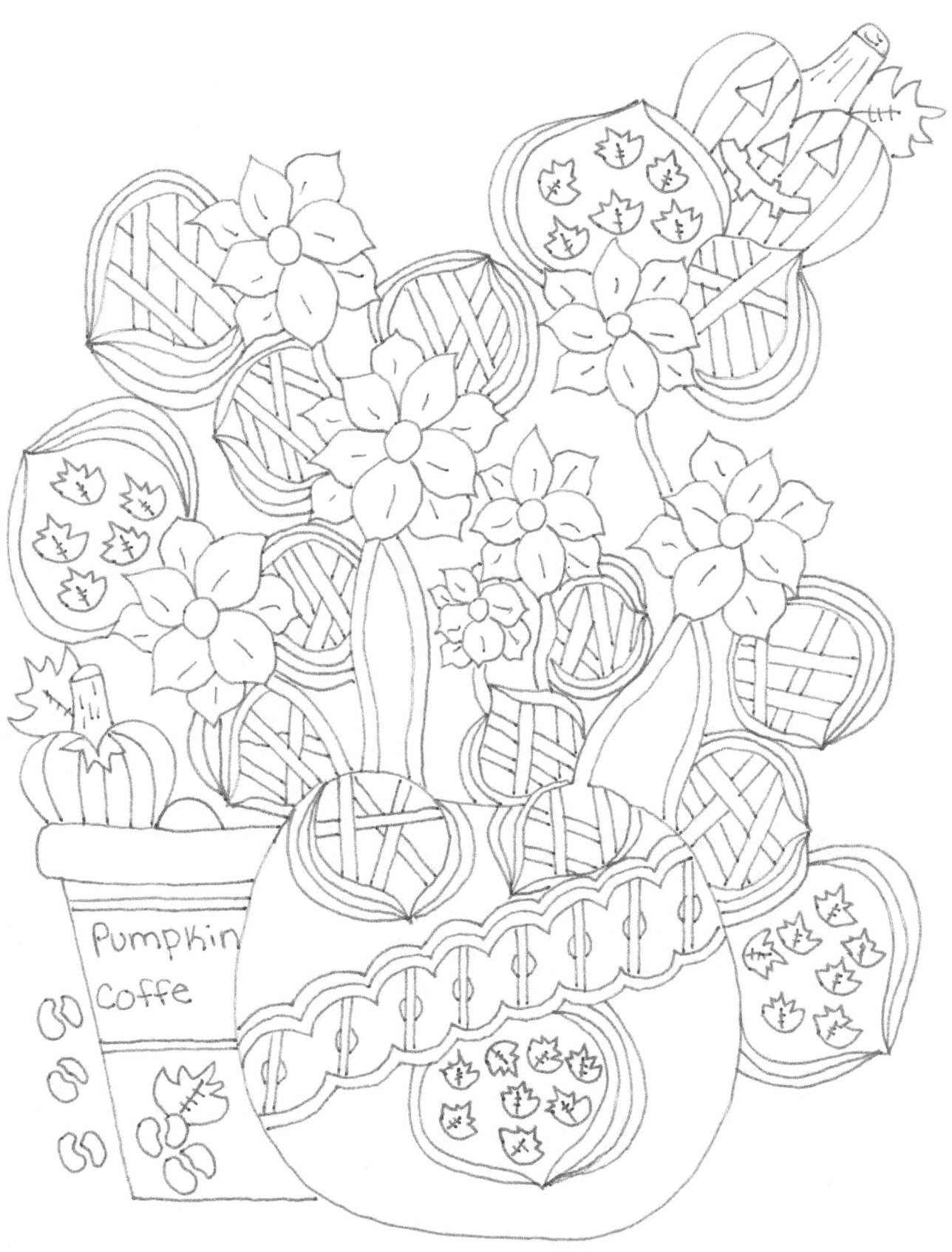

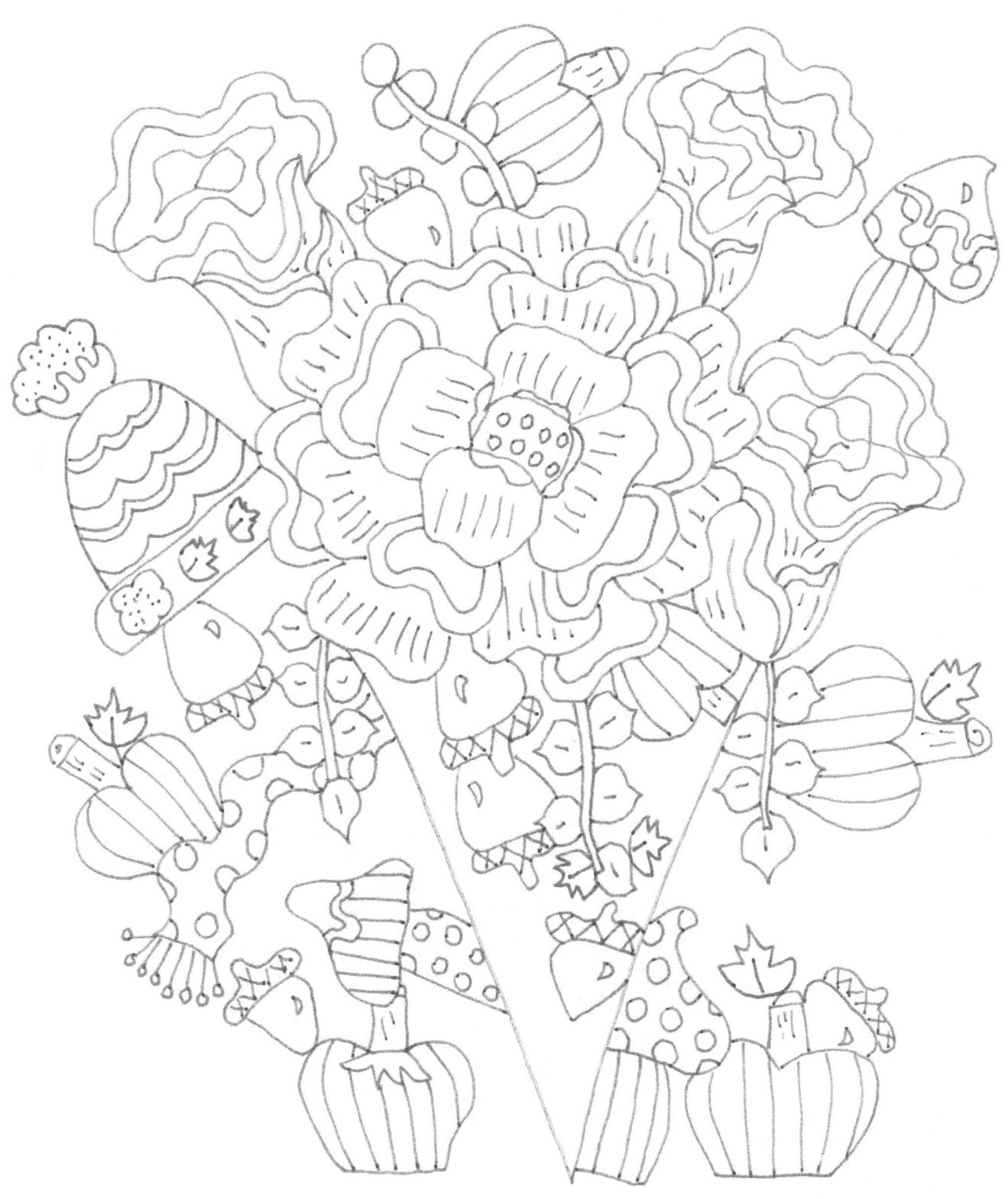

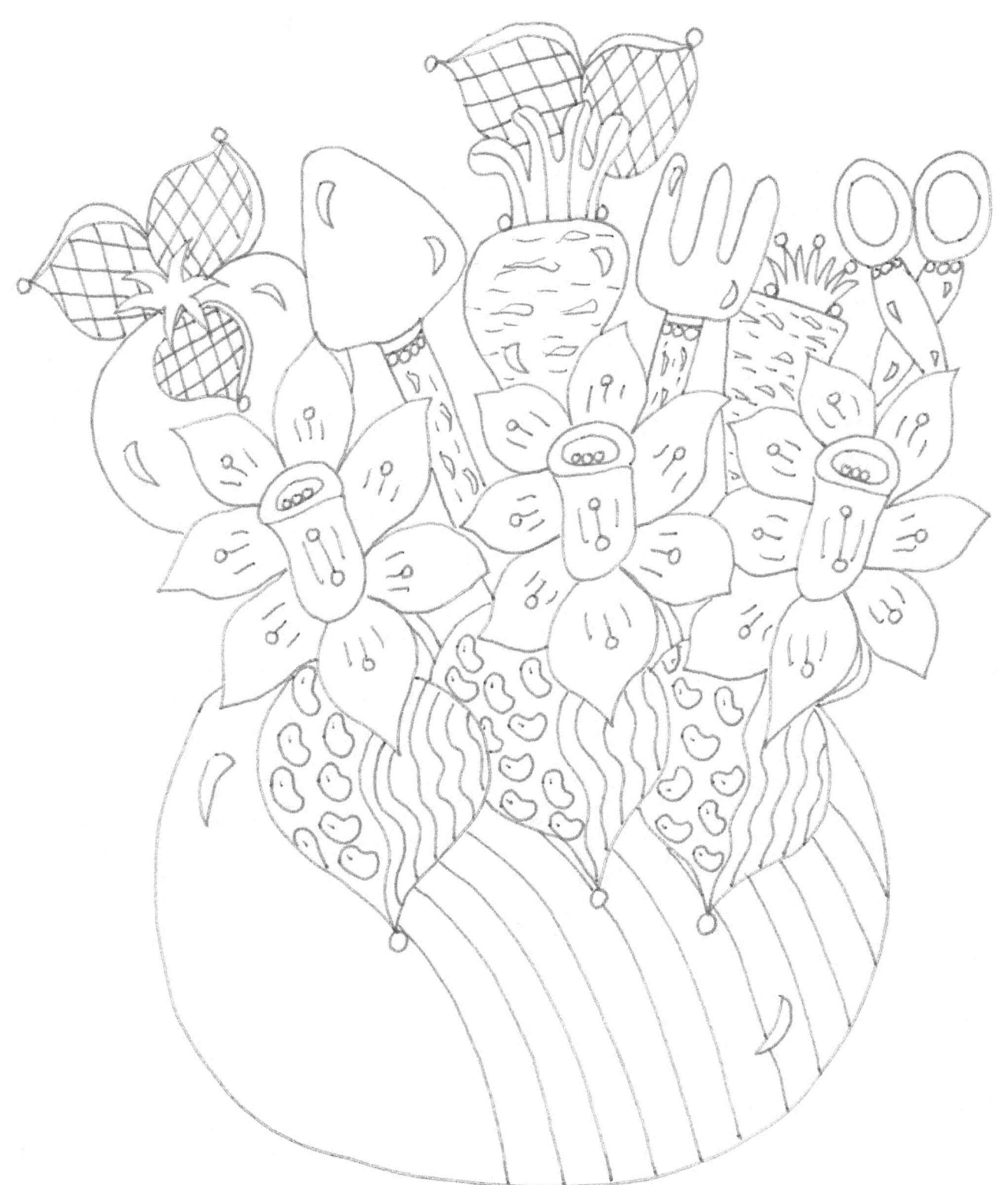

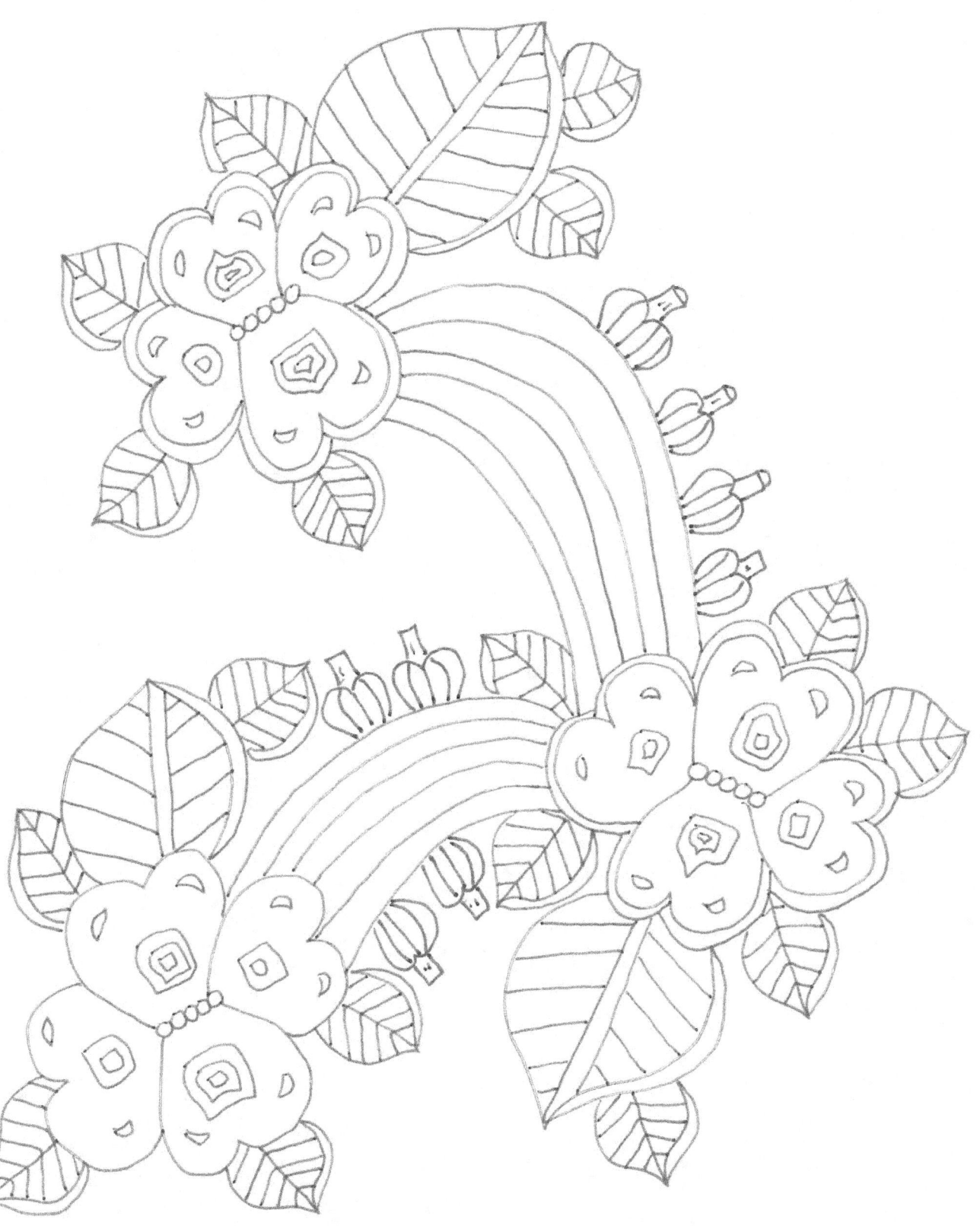

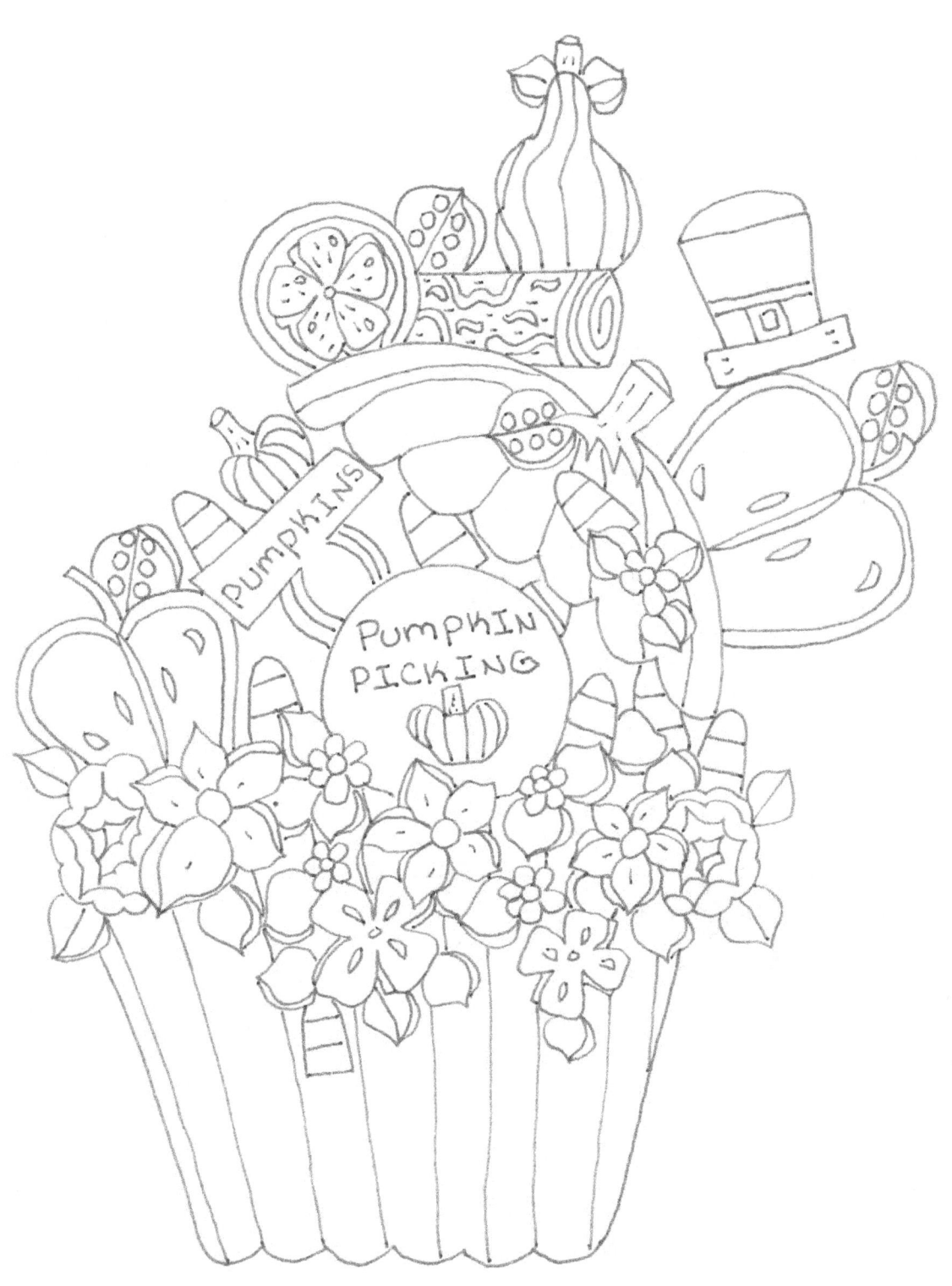

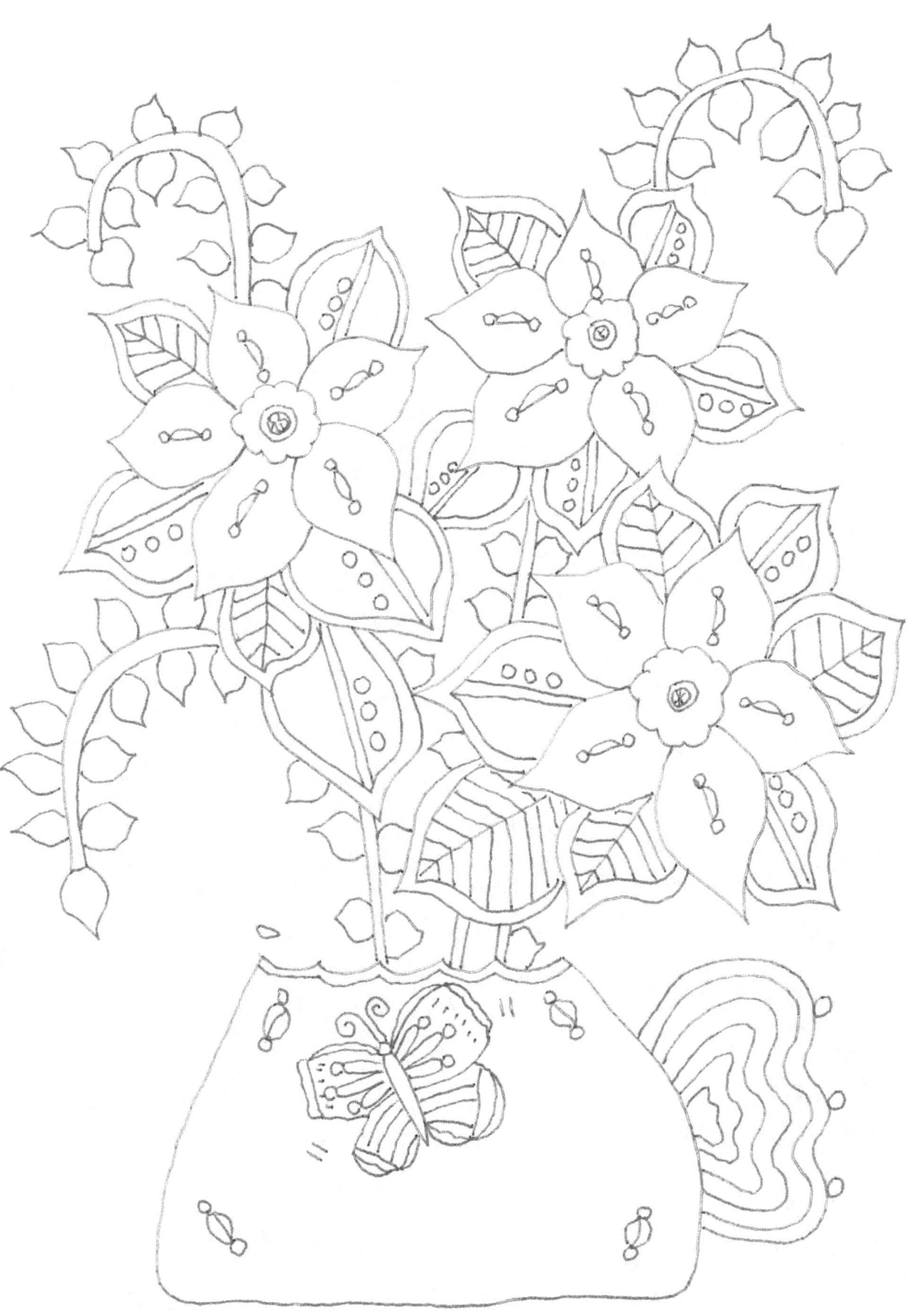

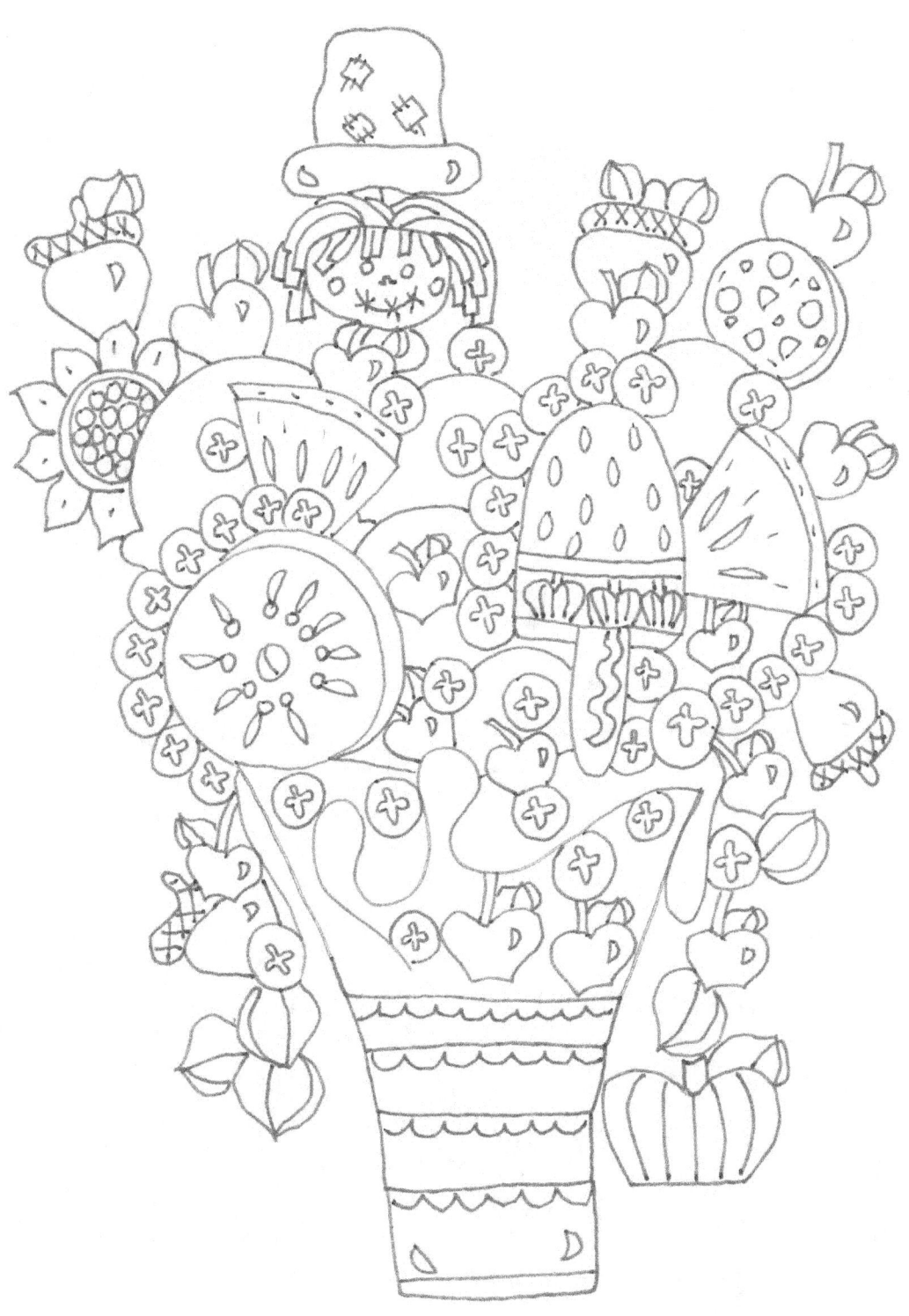

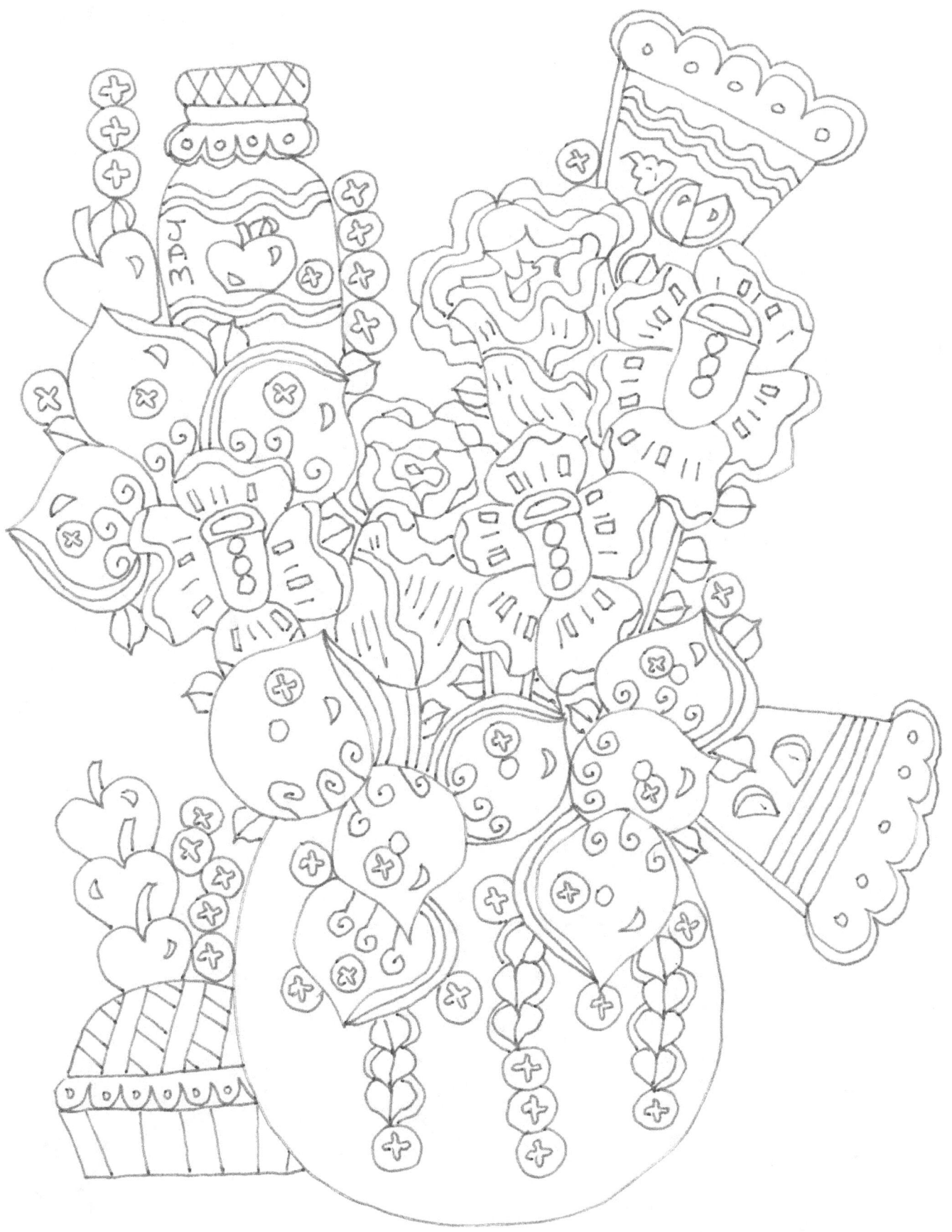

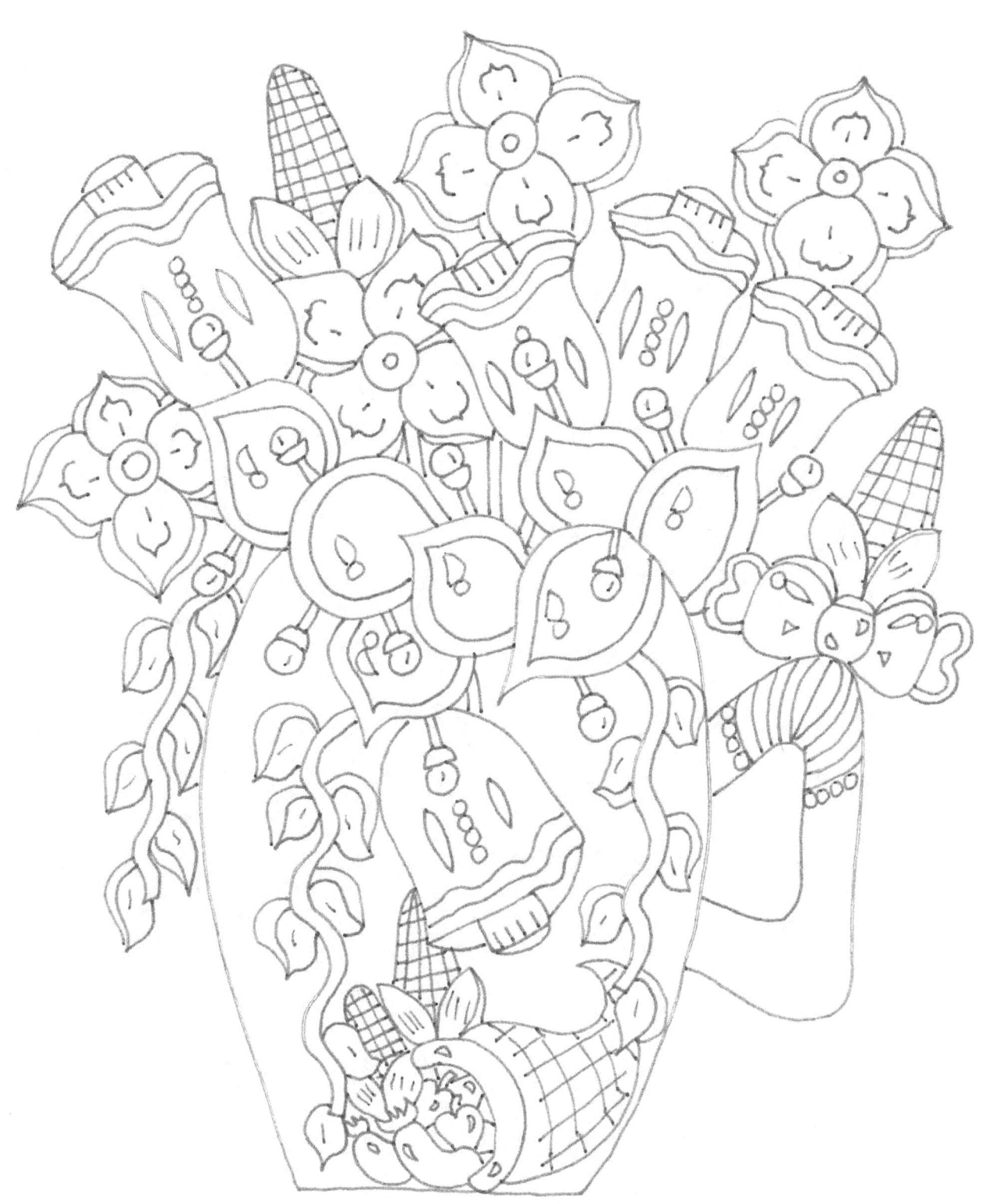

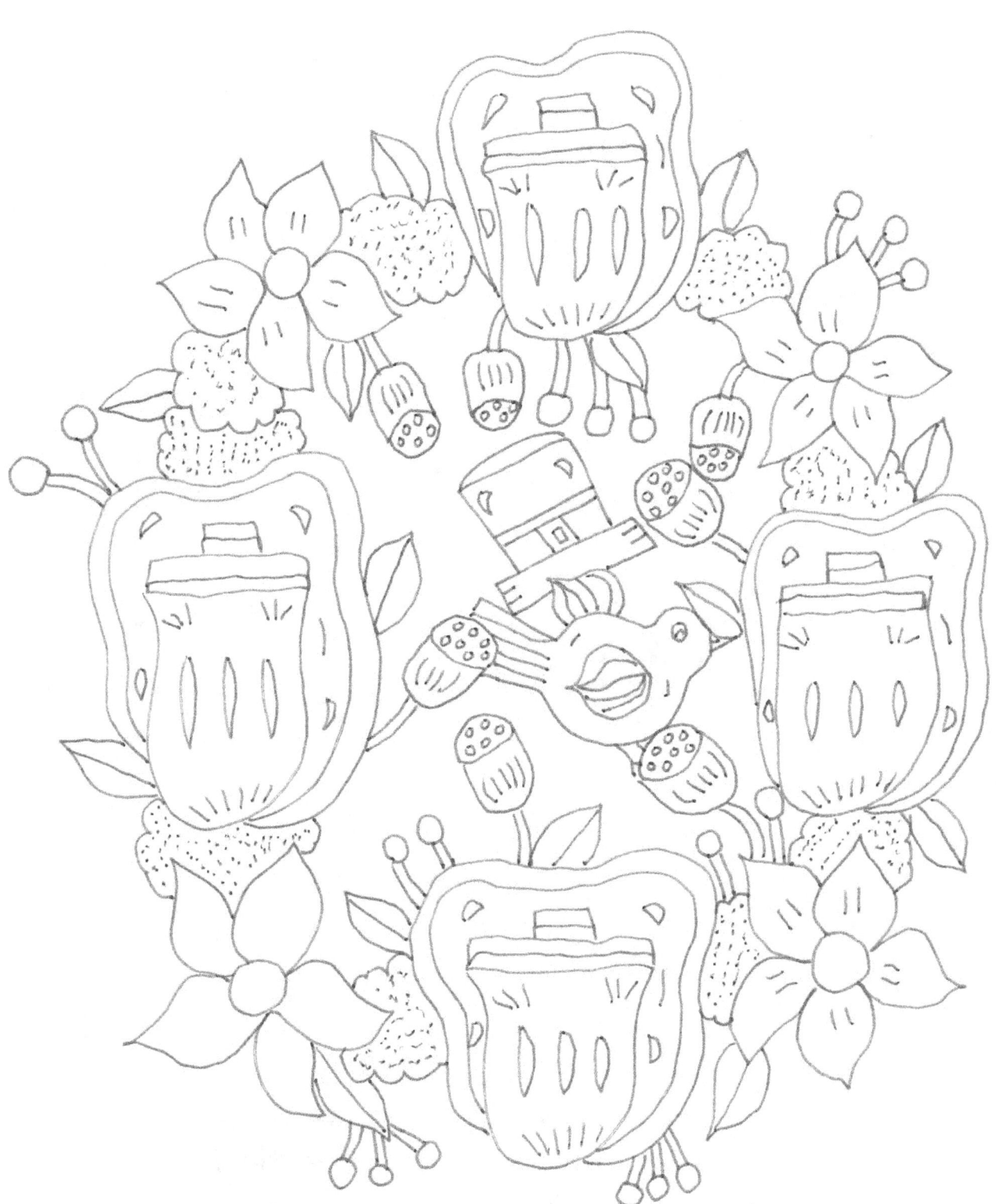

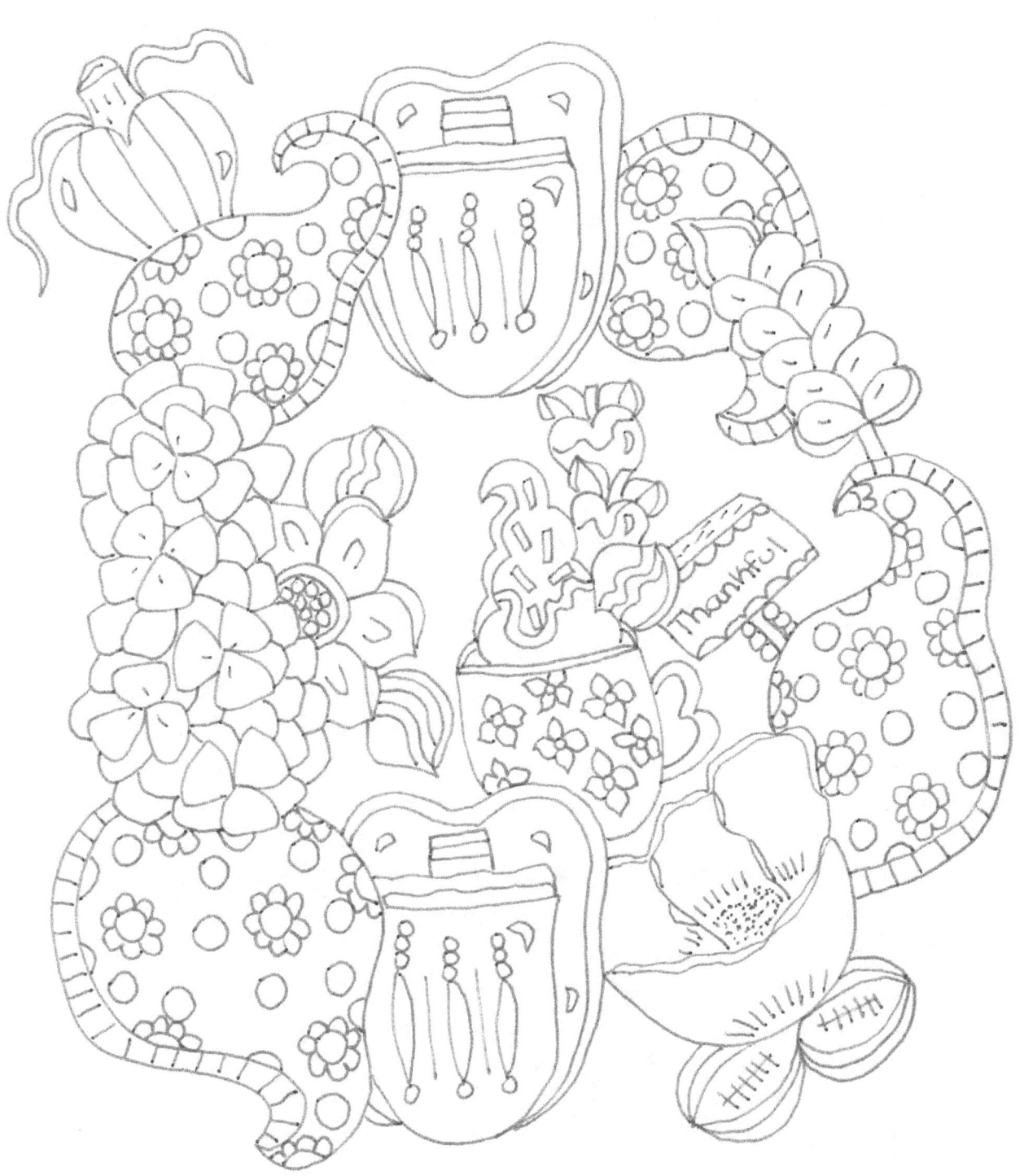

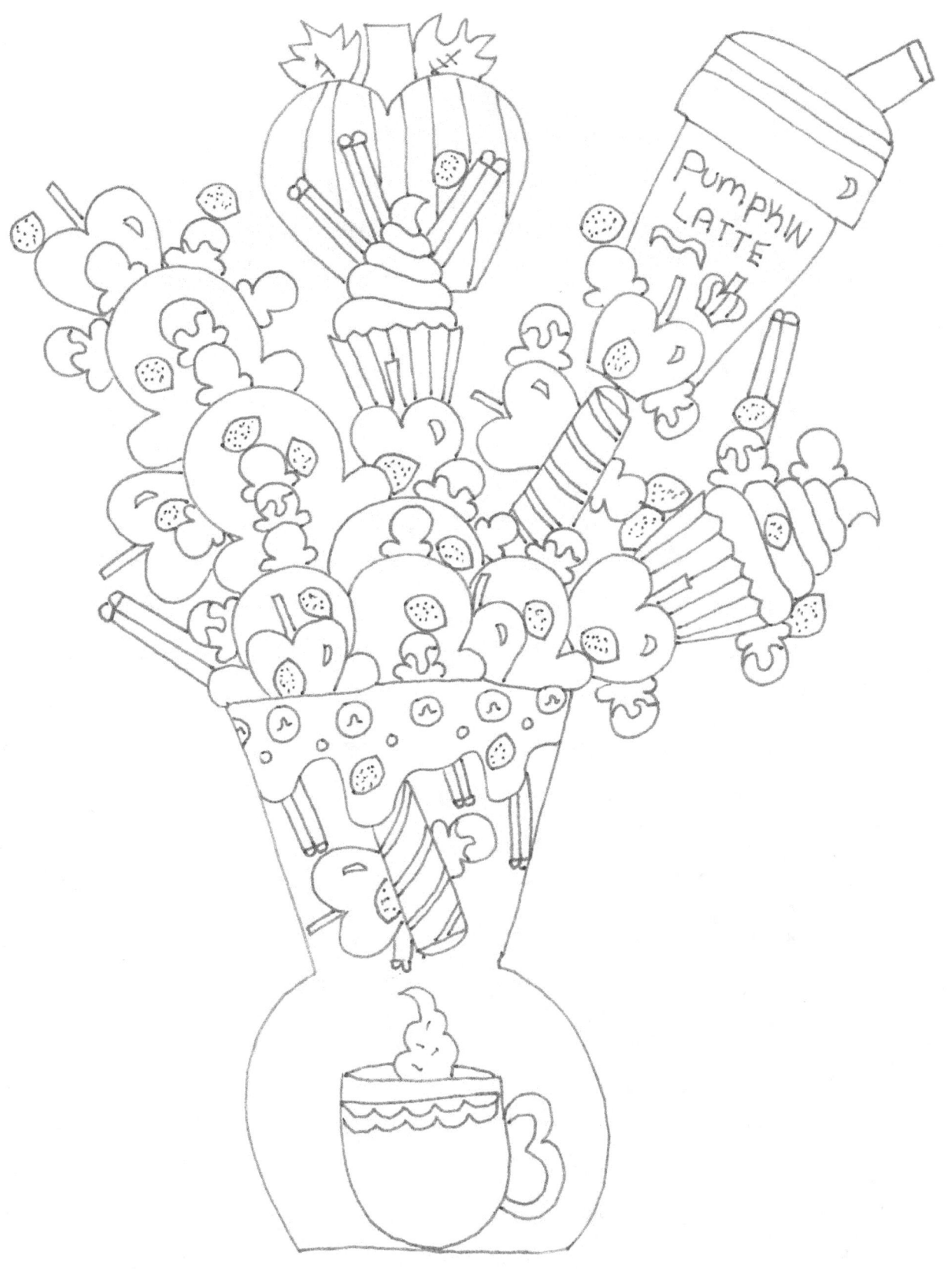

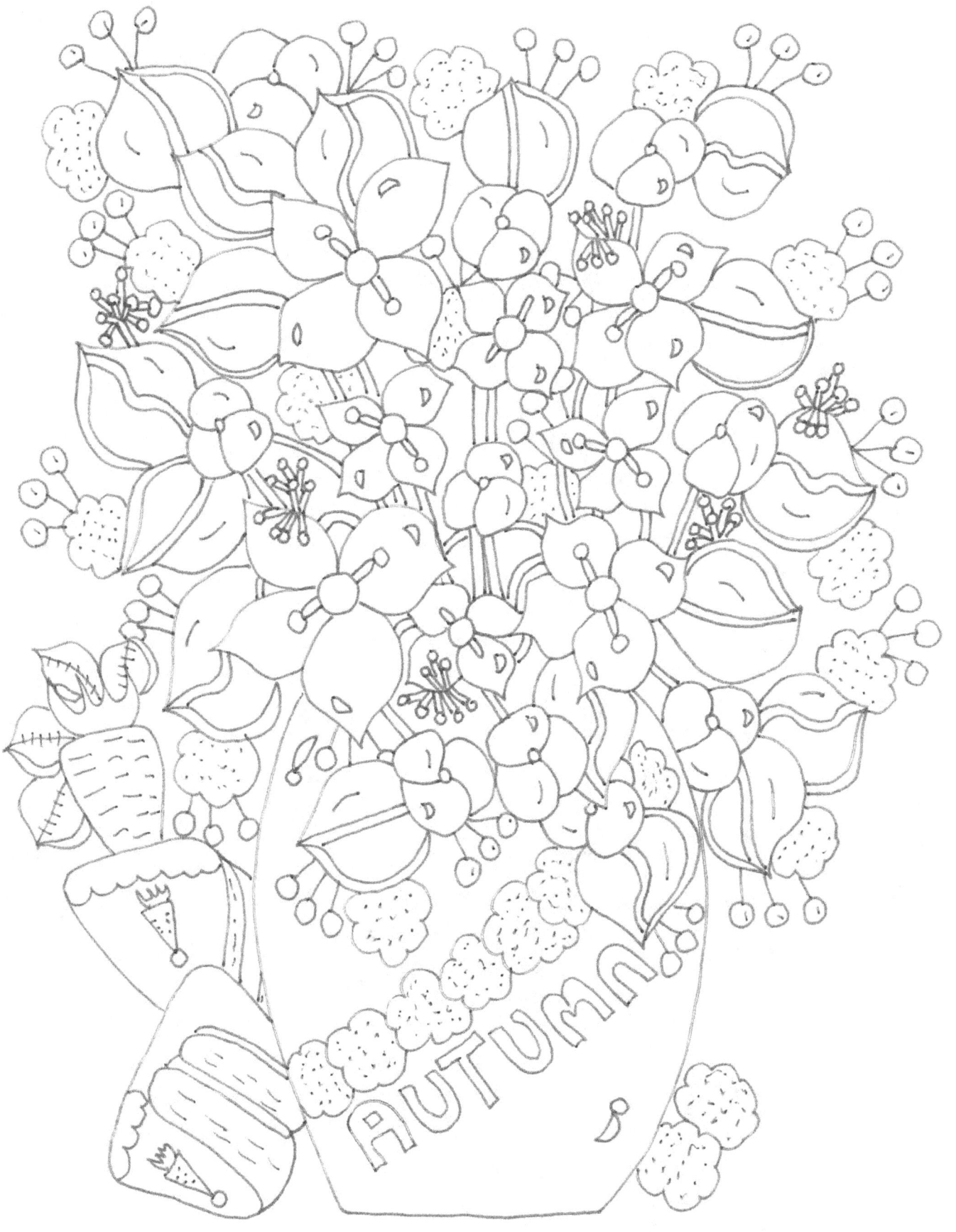

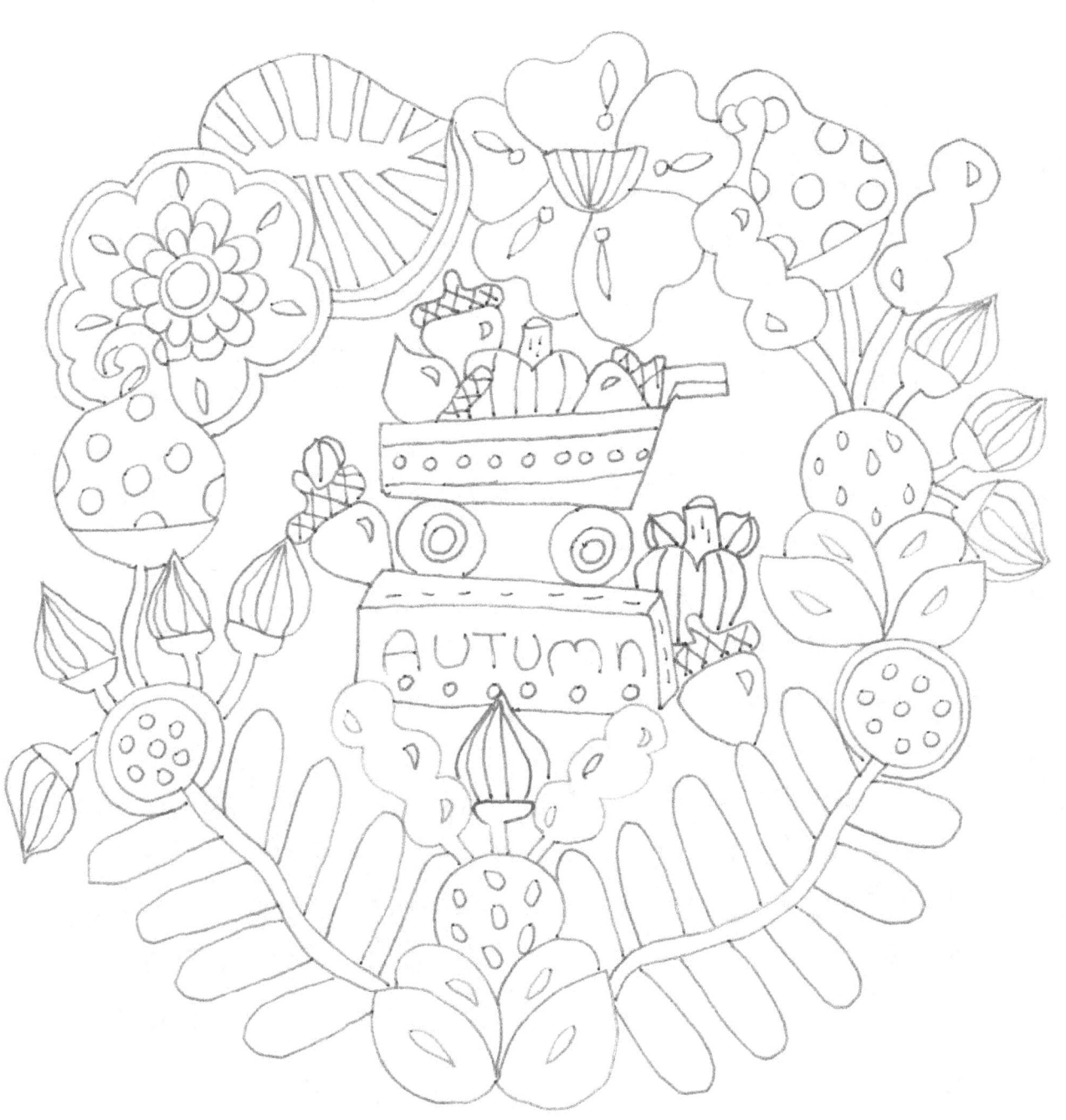

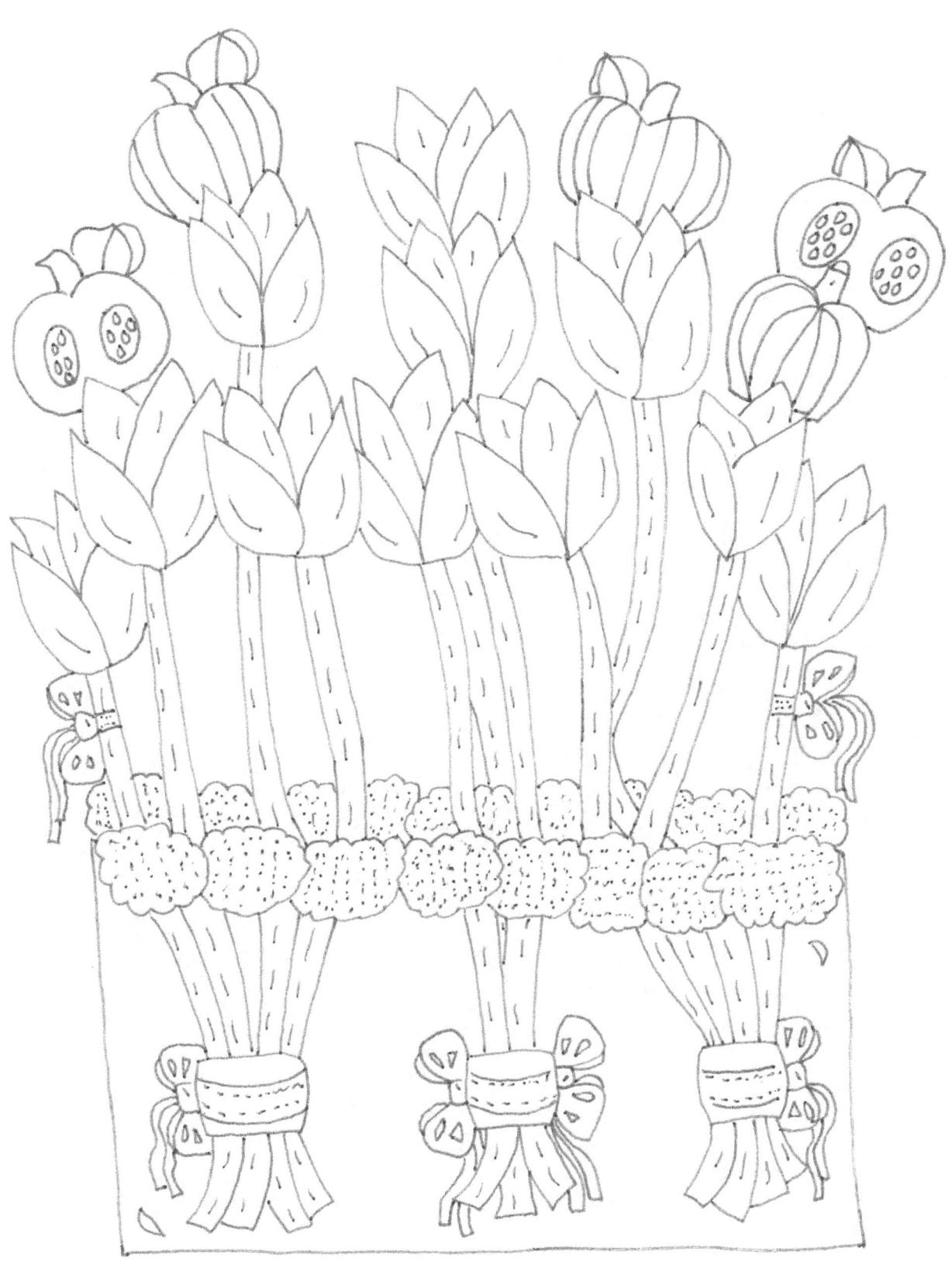

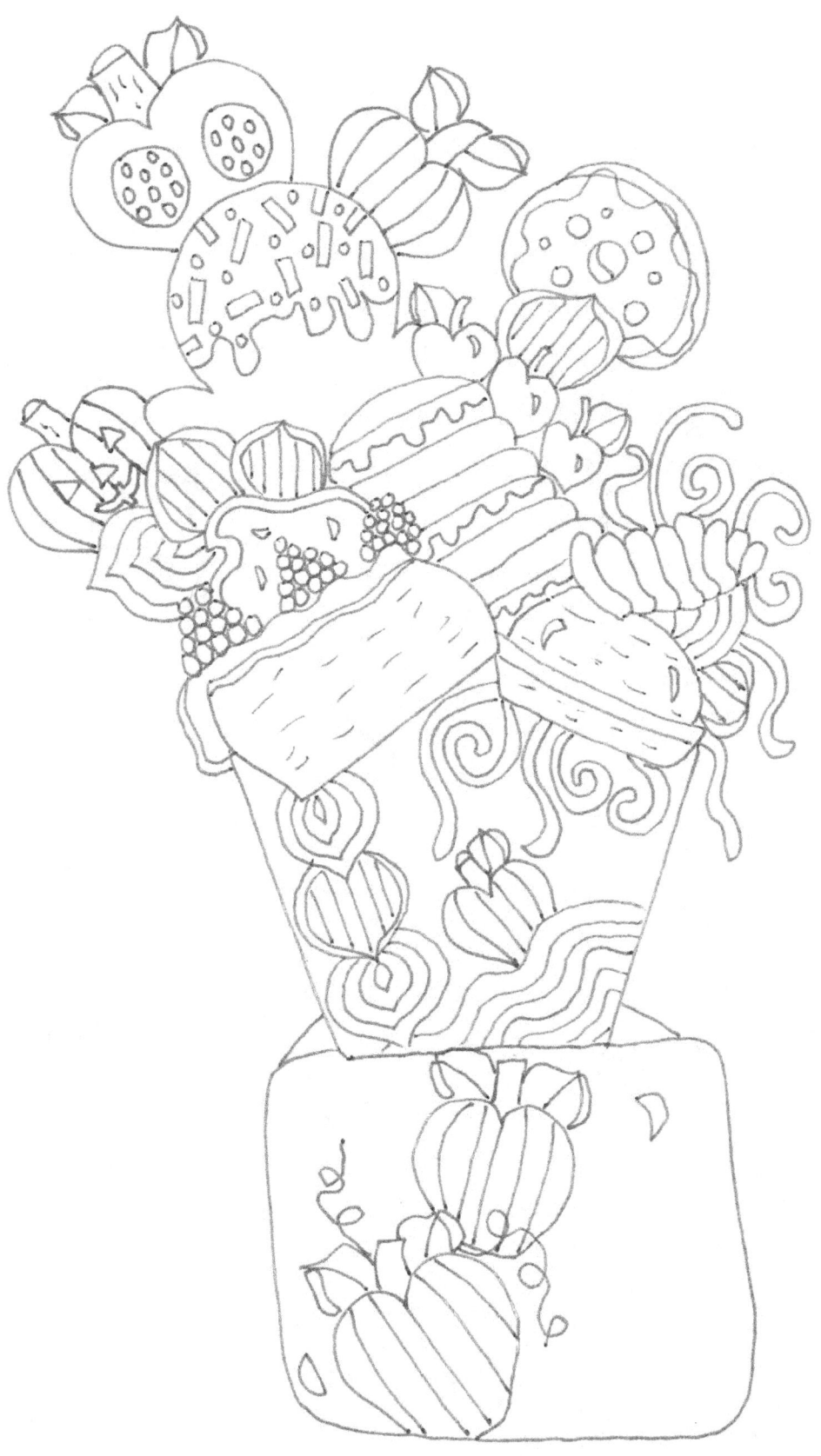

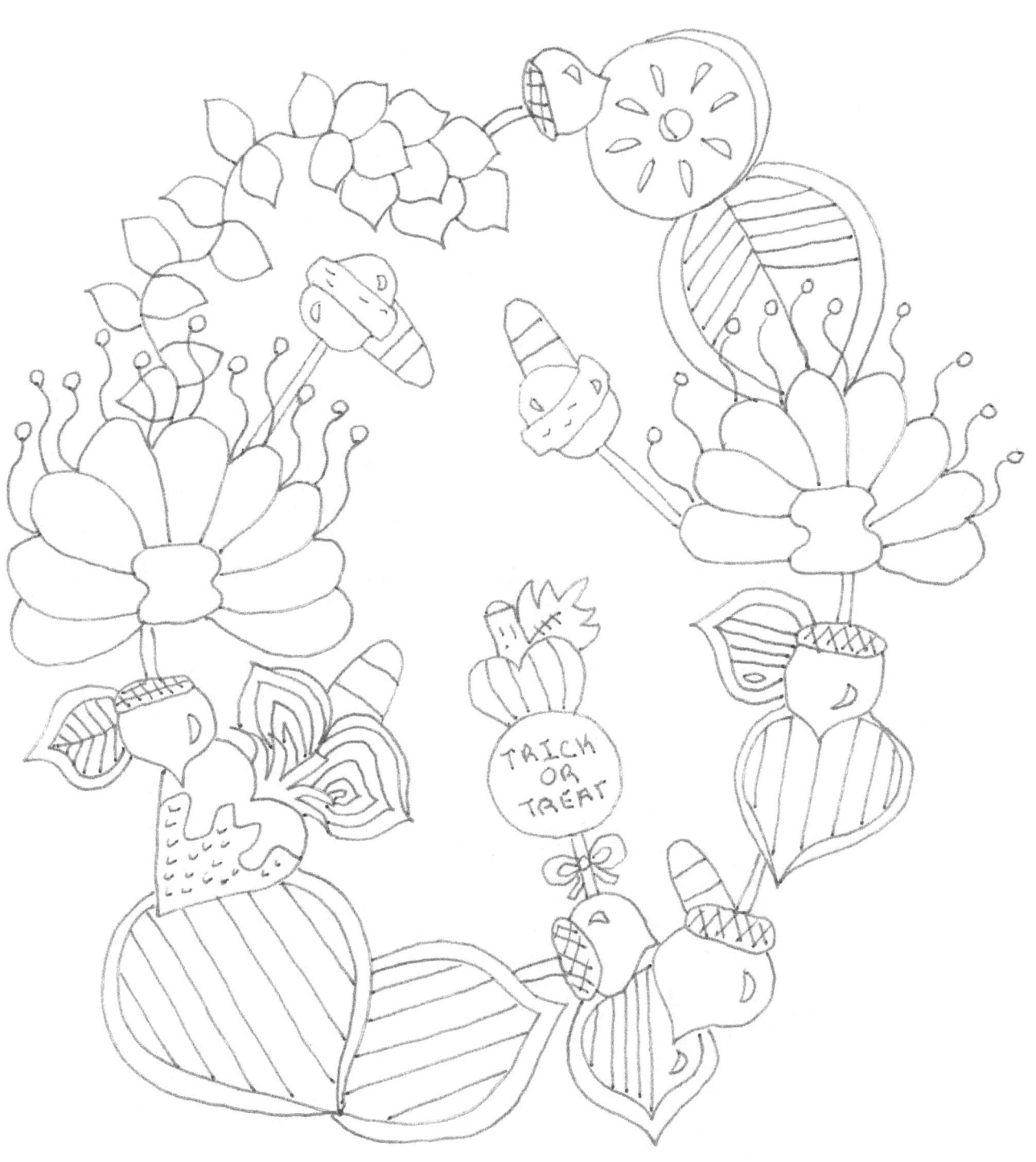

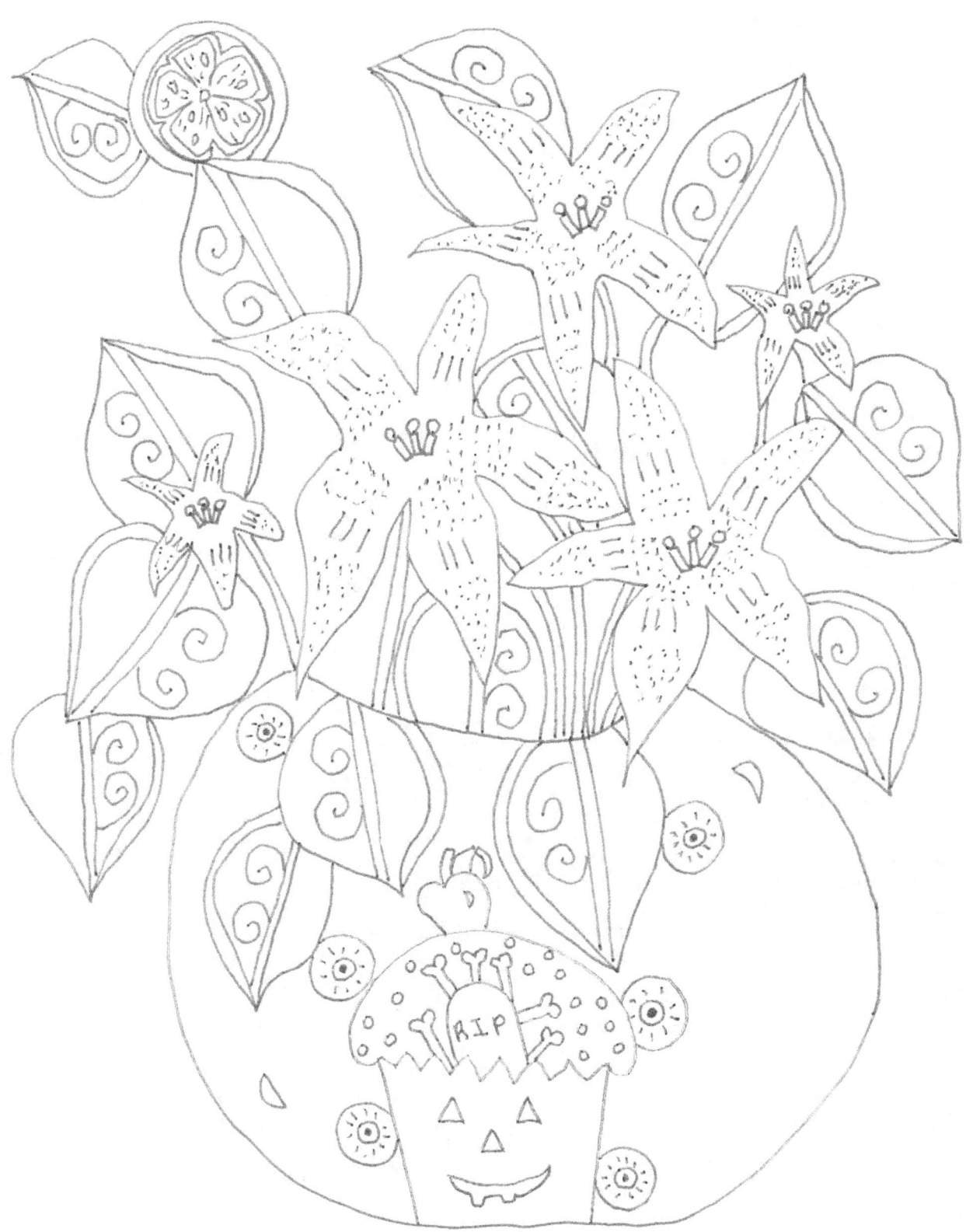

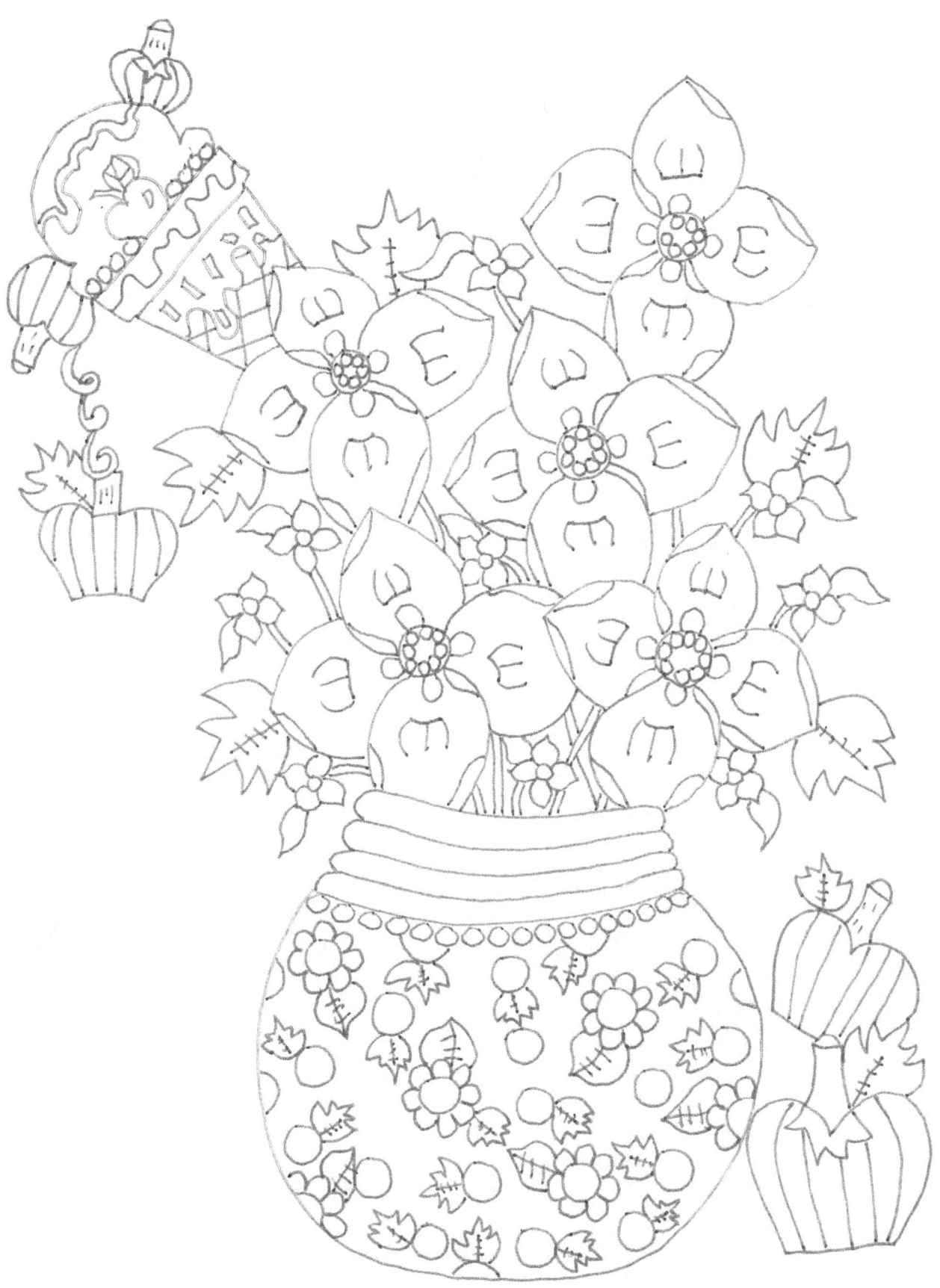

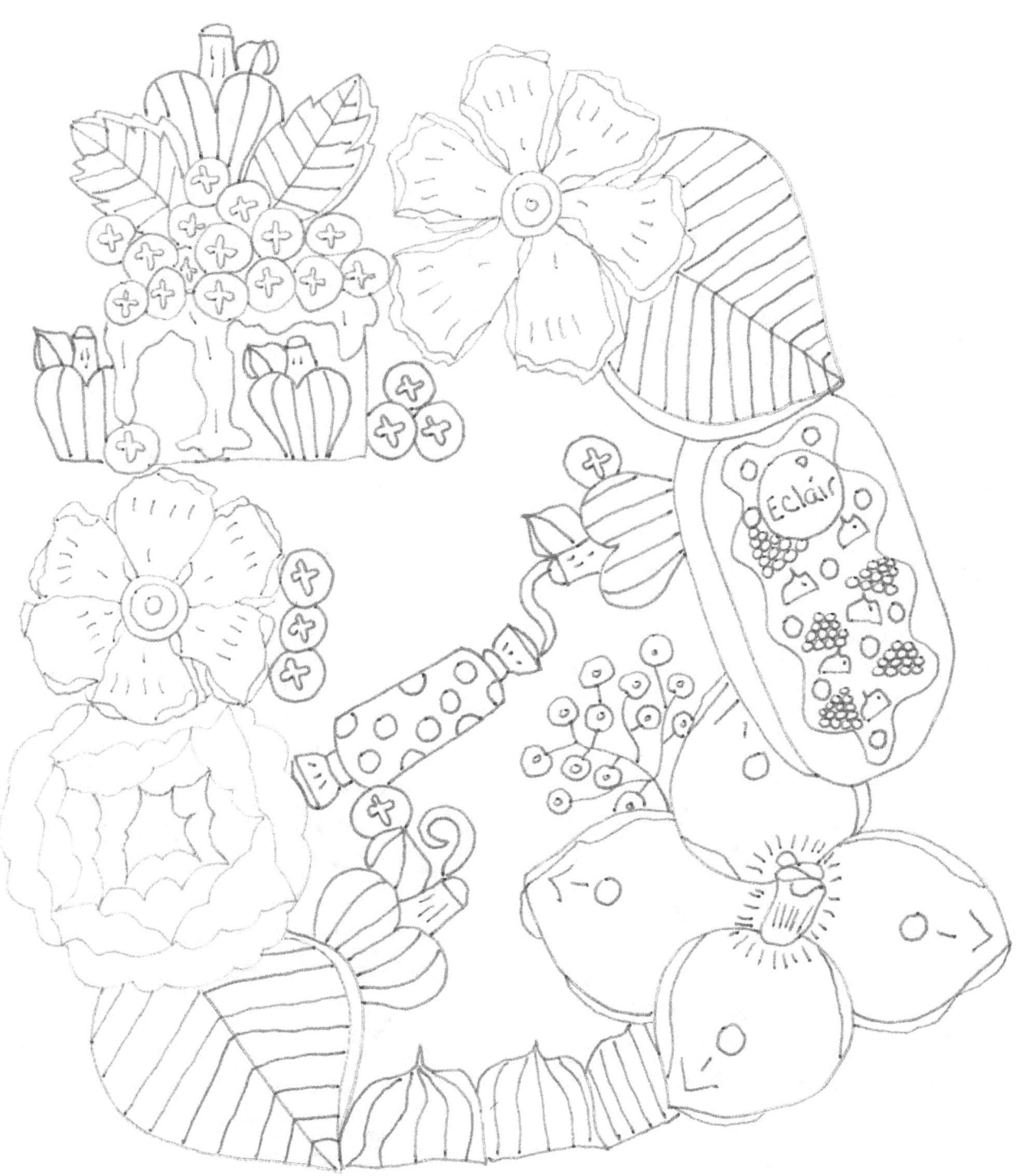

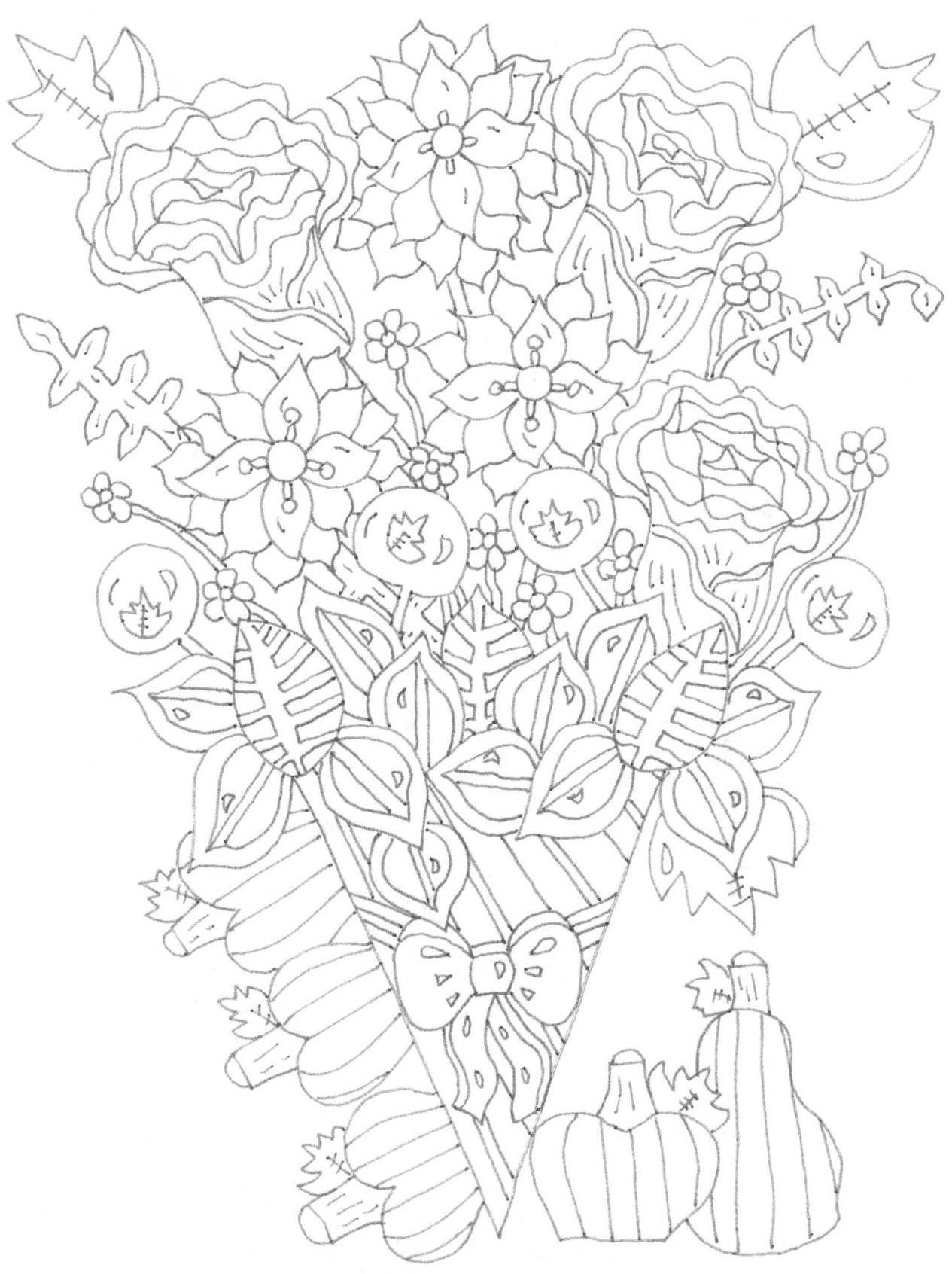

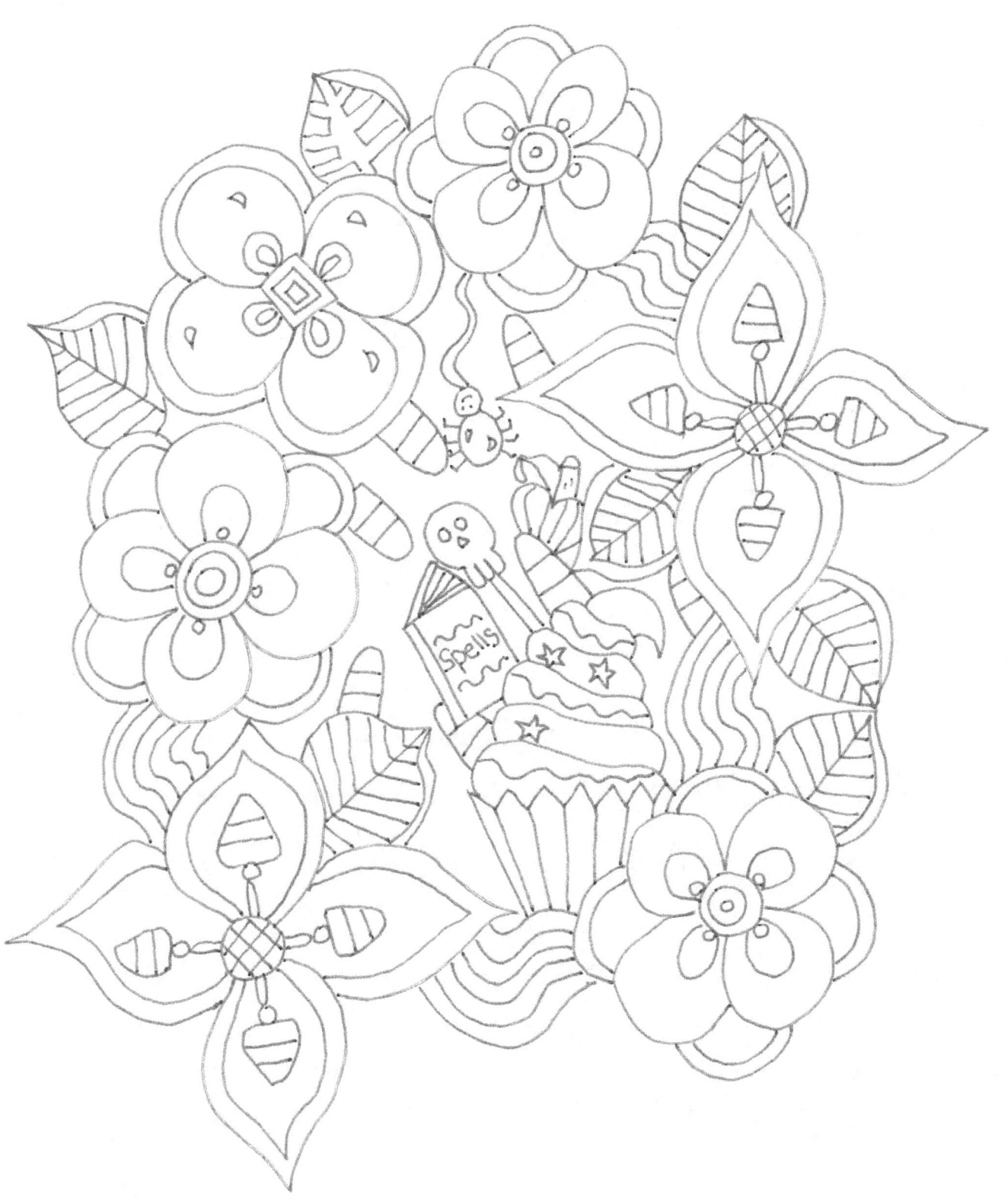

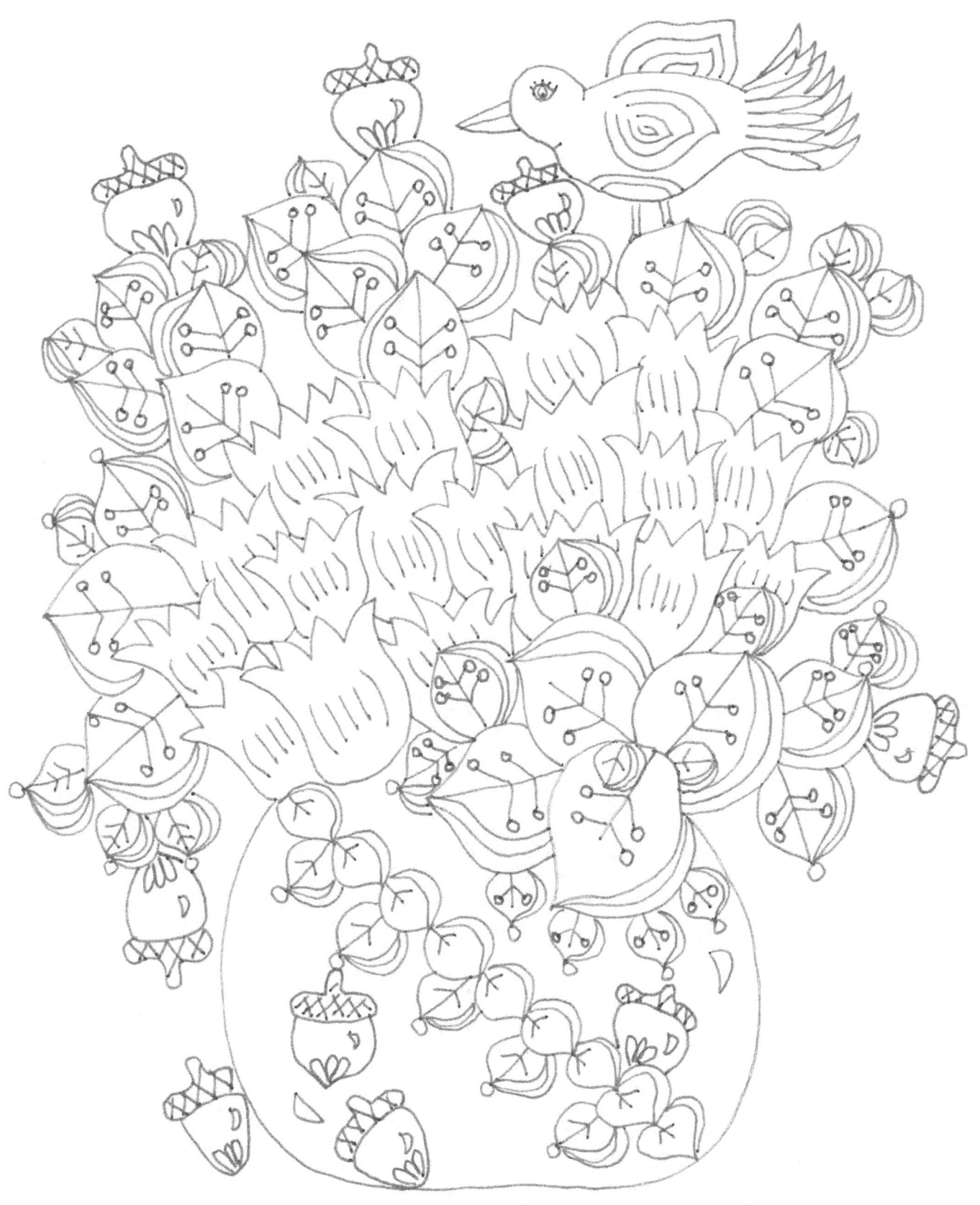

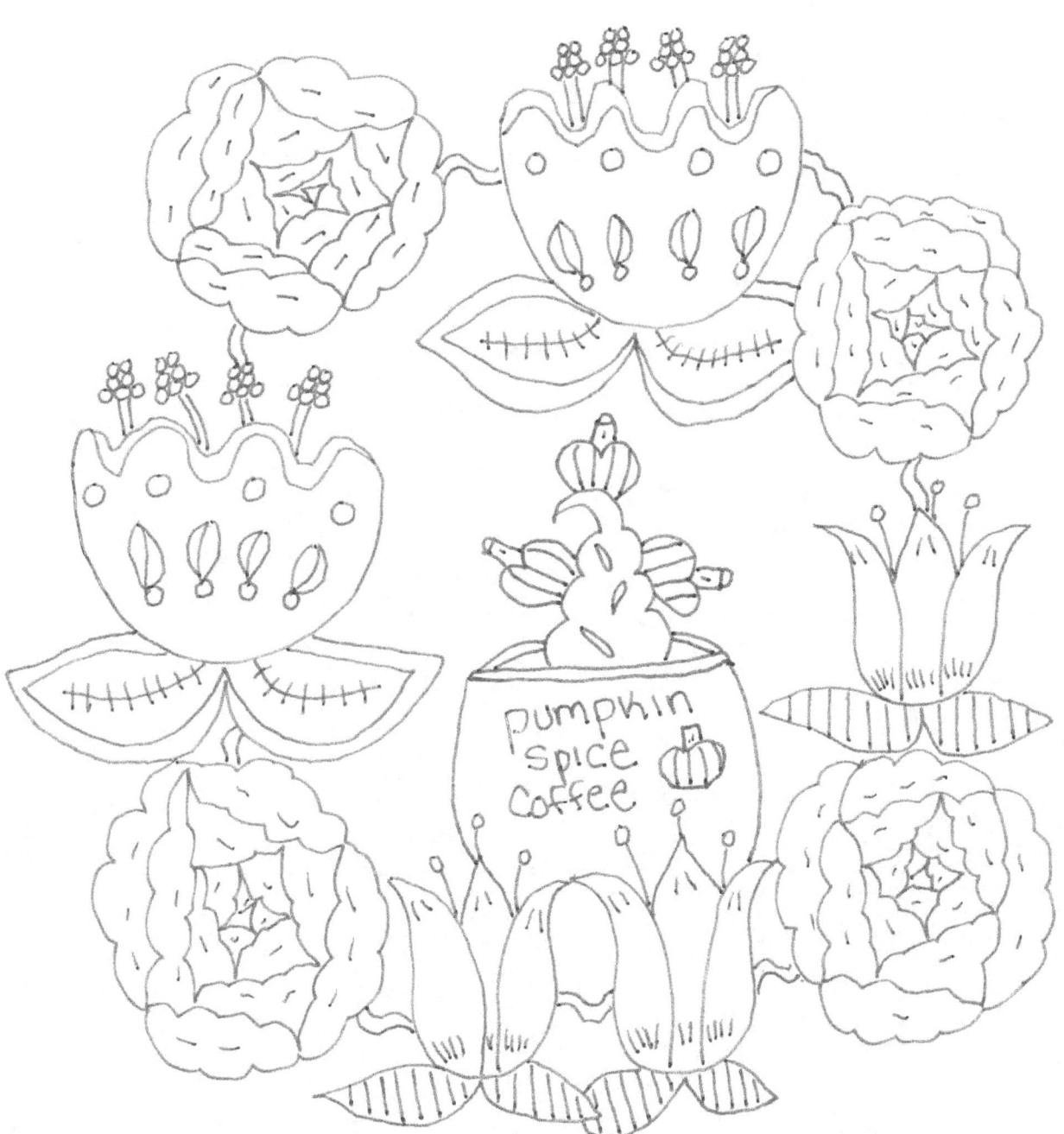

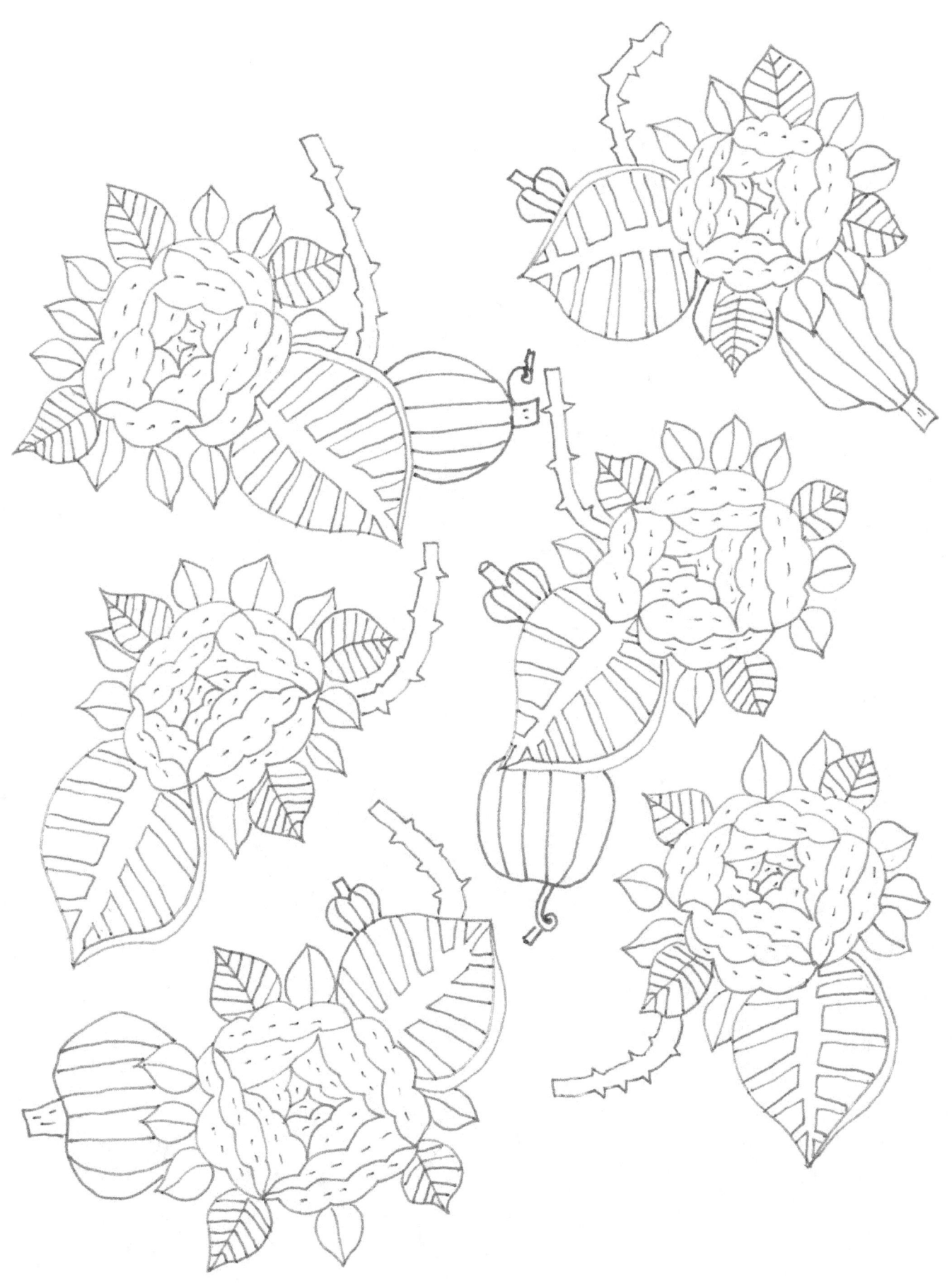

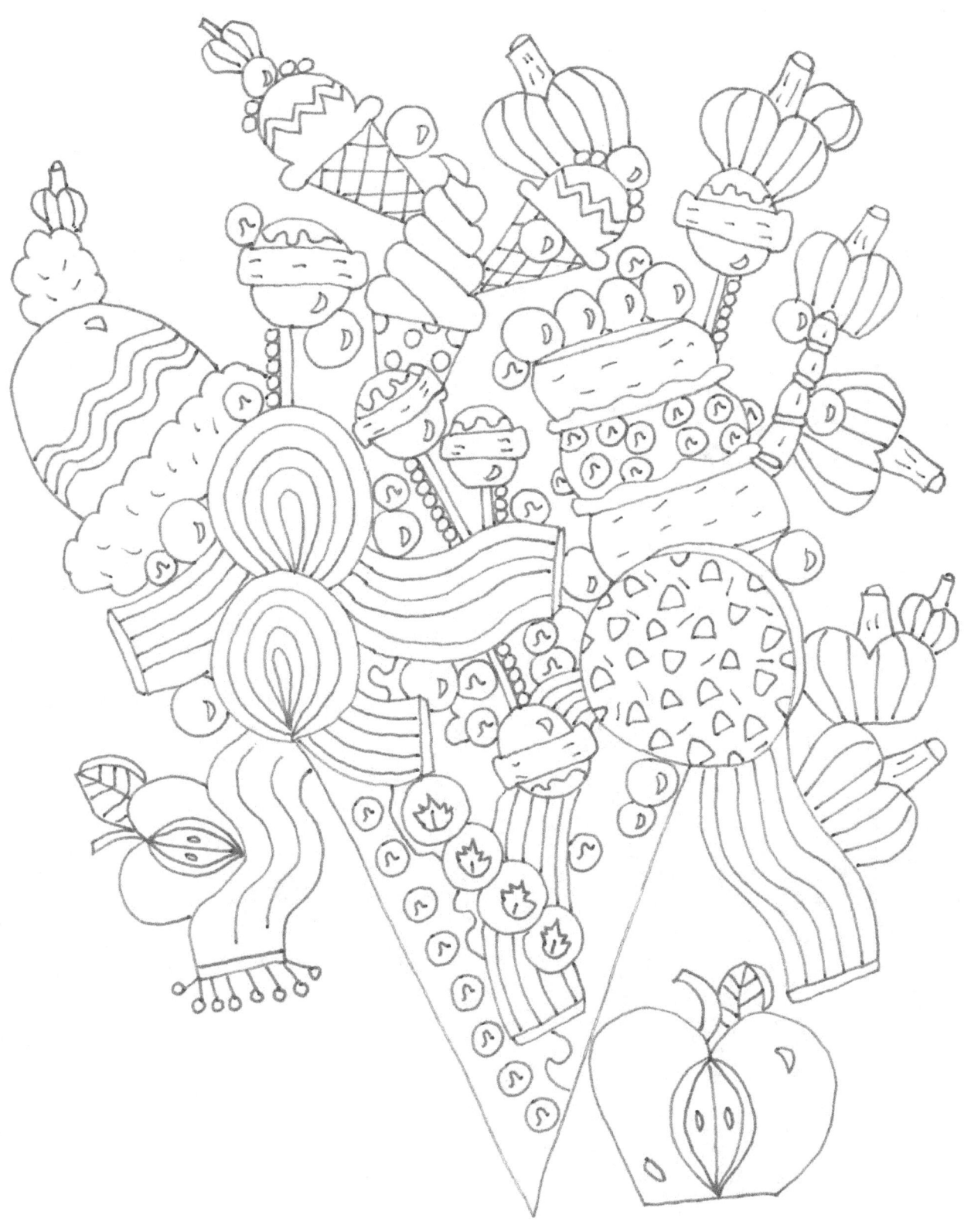

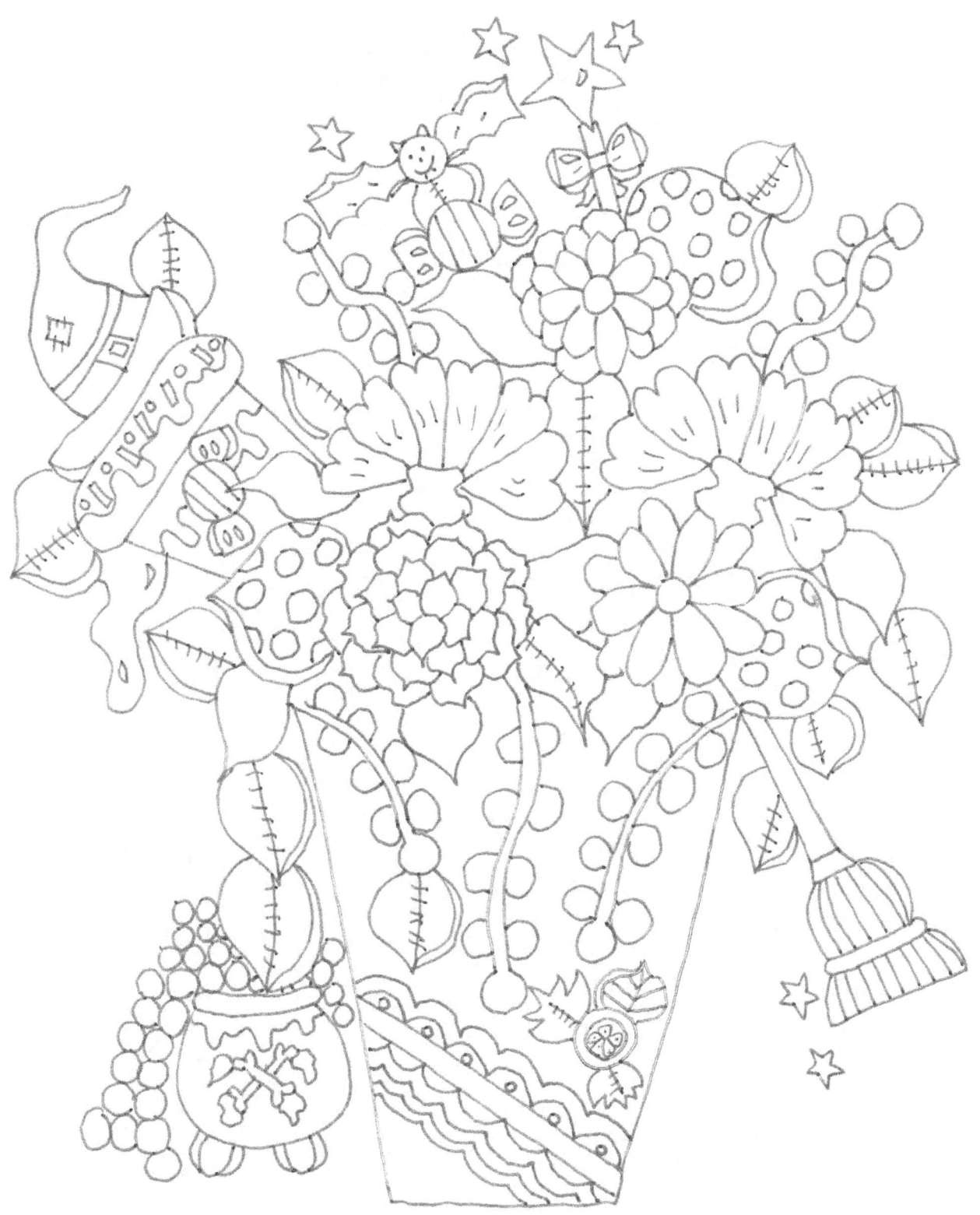

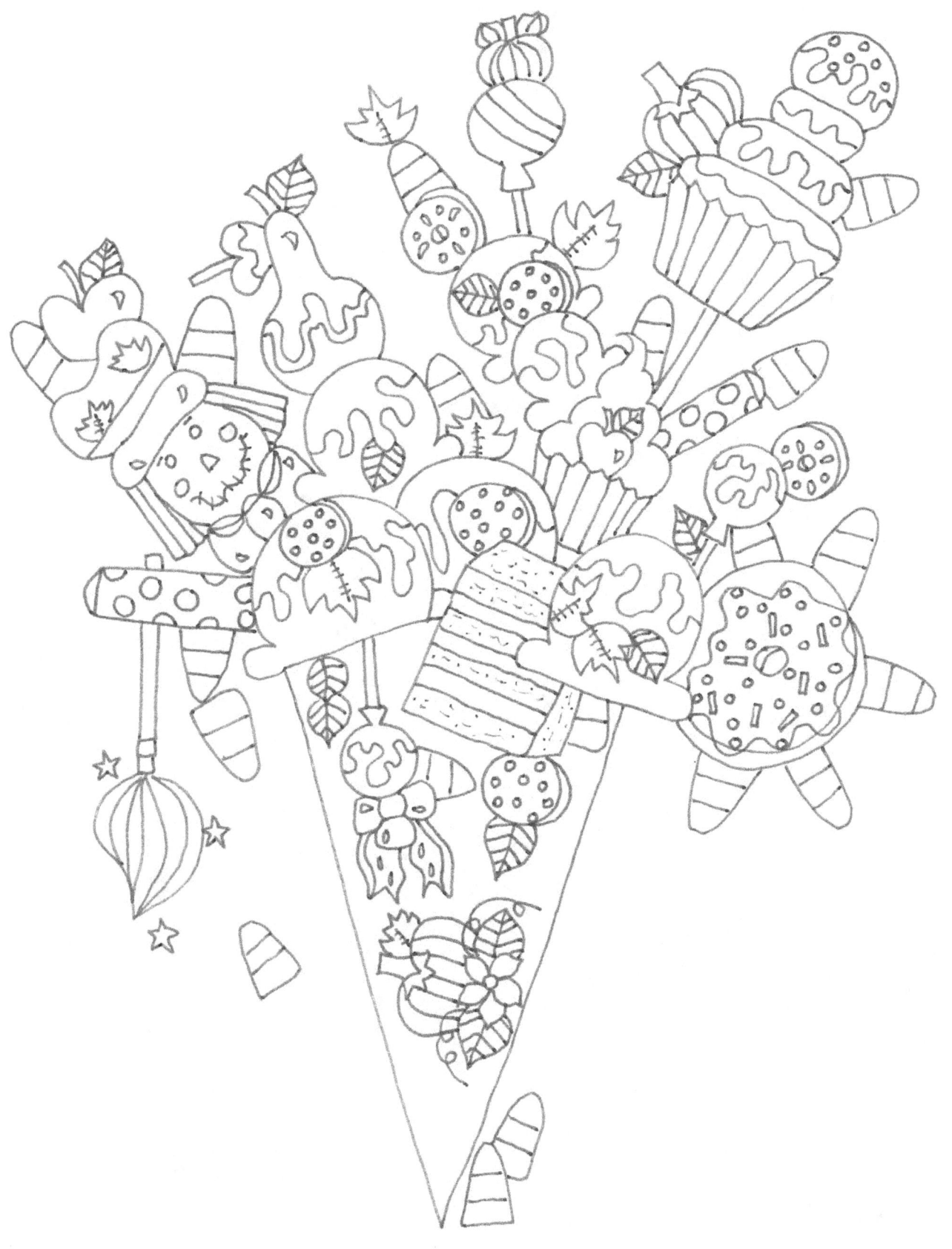

THANK YOU FOR PURCHASING AUTUMN BLESSINGS ADULT COLORING BOOK. YOU CAN CHECK OUT MY OTHER COLORING BOOKS LISTED BELOW WHICH CAN BE PURCHASED AT AMAZON.COM:

VINTAGE PARIS BAKE SHOP (Adult)
VINTAGE WINE GARDEN (Adult)
ICE CREAM MADNESS (Adult)
ICE CREAM MADNESS VOLUME 2 (Adult)
TEA & COFFEE TROPICAL TREASURES (Adult)
TEA & COFFEE OCEAN TREASURES (Adult)
TEA & COFFEE TREASURES (Adult)
BOTANICAL FLOWERS & MANDALAS (Adult)
MAJESTIC FALL (Adult)
A VERY RETRO CHRISTMAS (Adult)
MAGICAL DESSERTS (Kids)
MAGICAL DESSERTS VOLUME 2 (Kids)
MAGICAL DESSERTS VOLUME 3 (Kids)
FASHION DOLLS (Adult)
FAIRIES IN THE FLOWER GARDEN (Adult)
MERMAID'S WONDERLAND SEA OF ENCHANTMENT (Adult)
CHRISTMAS DESSERTS
VALENTINE'S DAYDREAMS COLORING BOOK (Adult)
VALENTINE'S DAY DELIGHTS (Adult)
VALENTINE'S FLOWERS & DESSERTS (Adult)
VALENTINE'S DAY DESSERTS (Adult)
VALENTINE'S DAY ANIMALS & Sweets (Kids)
VALENTINE DAY'S FLOWERS (Adult)
A VERY RUSTIC VALENTINE'S DAY (Adult)
ELEGANT FLOWERS (Adult)
ST. PATRICK'S DAY BLESSINGS (Adult)
A HAPPY ST. PATTY'S DAY (Kids)
ST. PATRICK'S DAY DESSERTS (Adult)
ST. PATRICK DAY FLOWERS (Adult)
SPRINGTIME FAIRIES (Adult)
SPECTACULAR DESSERTS (Adult)
BEAUTIFUL SPRINGTIME FLOWERS (Adult)
MERMAID DESSERTS (Adult)
FLORAL DELIGHTS (Adult)
FABULOUS SPRINGTIME WREATHS (Adult)
DELICIOUS SPRINGTIME DESSERTS (Adult)
CHARMING EASTER FLOWERS (Adult)
EASTER WONDERLAND (Adult)
EASTER BLESSINGS (Adult)
LOVELY EASTER WREATHS (Adult)
(Continued on next page)

EASTER BASKETS (Adult)
GORGEOUS SPRINGTIME FLOWERS (Adult)
MARVELOUS SPRINGTIME FLOWERS (Adult)
MAGNIFICENT FLOWERS (Adult)
WINTER FLOWERS (Adult)
WINTER BLOOMS (Adult)
TROPICAL FLOWERS (Adult)
VALENTINE'S DAY BOUQUET (Adult)
VALENTINE'S DAY SWEETS (Adult)
VALENTINE'S DAY FARMHOUSE FLOWERS (Adult)
ST. PATTY'S DAY FLOWERS & SHENANIGANS (Adult)
LUCKY ST. PATTY'S DAY FLOWERS (Adult)
ST. PATTY'S DAY BOUQUETS (Adult)
ST. PATRICK'S DAY SWEETS (Adult)
SPRING WREATHS & FLOWERS (Adult)
ST. PATRICK'S DAY BLESSINGS: 2 (Adult)
VINTAGE SPRING FLOWERS (Adult)
SWEET SPRING FLOWERS (Adult)
SPRING FLOWERS (Adult)
EASTER FLOWERS (Adult)
EASTER SWEETS (Adult)
FARMHOUSE FLOWERS (Adult)
MOTHER'S DAY WREATHS (Adult)
FLOWERY WREATHS (Adult)
FLORAL DESSERTS (Adult)
DELICIOUS DESSERTS (Adult)
SUMMERTIME FLOWERS (Adult)
WILD DESSERTS (Adult)
SUMMER BLOSSOMS (Adult)
RUSTIC FARMHOUSE FLOWERS (Adult)
SUMMER DESSERTS (Adult)
GOURMET ICE CREAM CONES (Adult)
ICE CREAM CONES DELIGHTS (Adult)
FARMER'S MARKET FLOWERS (Adult)
FALL FLOWERS (Adult)
AUTUMN WREATHS (Adult)
FALL DESSERTS (Adult)
AUTUMN DESSERTS (Adult)
HALLOWEEN DESSERTS (Adult)

IF YOU ENJOYED YOUR COLORING EXPERIENCE, PLEASE TELL OTHERS ABOUT IT BY WRITING A REVIEW ON AMAZON.COM UNDER THE BOOK YOU COLORED.

www.ingramcontent.com/pod-product-compliance
Lightning Source LLC
Chambersburg PA
CBHW080527220526
45465CB00006B/2621